ESSAYS ON THE TRIAL OF GALILEO

BY

Richard S. Westfall
Indiana University

1989

Vatican Observatory Publications
Special Series: *Studi Galileiani*

Distributed (except in Italy and Vatican City State) by:

> THE UNIVERSITY OF NOTRE DAME PRESS
> Notre Dame, Indiana 46556
> USA

Distributed in Italy and the Vatican City State by:

> LIBRERIA EDITRICE VATICANA
> V— 00120 CITTÀ DEL VATICANO
> VATICAN CITY STATE

ISBN 0-268-00923-6

CONTENTS

FOREWORD

On March 5, 1615, the Congregation of the Index banned Copernicus's *De revolutionibus* on the grounds that it defended "the false Pythagorean doctrine that the earth moves and the sun is motionless", a doctrine "altogether contrary to Holy Scripture". In February 1632, Galileo published his *Dialogue on Two Chief World Systems*, in which he strongly defended the Copernican world-view. In April 1633, he was brought to trial before the Holy Office in Rome, and charged with violating an injunction said to be officially conveyed to him by Cardinal Bellarmine in 1616 not to "hold, teach, or defend in any way whatsoever" the banned Copernican doctrine, and with concealing the existence of this injunction during the negotiations that preceded the publication of the *Dialogue*. Galileo produced a certificate given to him by Bellarmine in 1616 stating that he had been officially notified of the decree banning Copernicus's work, but that no other action had been taken against him. On June 22, Galileo was condemned, "on vehement suspicion of heresy", for having held and defended as probable "a doctrine which is false and contrary to Holy Scripture". The *Dialogue* was banned; Galileo was forced to abjure the heresy that "the sun is the center of the world and motionless and that the earth is not the center and moves". He was sentenced to perpetual house-arrest.

This is the bare outline of the most famous episode in all of the long and complicated history of the interactions between religion and natural science, an outline which has been filled in over the years in so many different ways and in so many different colors. The story still elicits an immediate emotional response today, on the part of believer and non-believer alike. For many, it came to symbolize a radical antagonism between free inquiry and the demands of religious faith. To others, it has been a reminder of human weakness, a memorial of a conflict that might never have occurred had the cast of characters or the time of the action been ever so slightly different. To Catholic scientists, it has been a particular source of unease, recalling a wrong turning taken at a crucial moment in the development of modern science.

In an address to the Pontifical Academy of Sciences in November 1979, shortly after he became Pope, John Paul II acknowledged this unease and the need to make amends.[1] The occasion was the centenary of Einstein's birth. "The greatness of Galileo is known to all, as is that of Einstein", the Pope declared. But the difference between the two, he went on, is that Galileo "had much to suffer -- we cannot disguise it -- from the representatives and institutions of the Church". He recalled a passage in *Gaudium et Spes*, one of the major documents of the Second Vatican Council, deploring the attitudes of Christians who in the past "did not show themselves sufficiently aware of the legitimate autonomy of science".

The Pope expressed himself as desirous of "going beyond" the position taken by the Council. "I want theologians, scientists, and historians, animated by a desire for honest collaboration, to deepen their study of the Galileo case, and in a frank recognition of wrongs done, from whichever side they may have come, to remove the barriers to a fruitful relation of science and faith that the Galileo affair still raises in many minds. I give my wholehearted support to that effort which could honor the truth of faith and of science alike, and open the door to their future collaboration."

And he went on to quote approvingly from Galileo's celebrated *Letter to the Grand Duchess Christina* (1615), in which Galileo attempted to persuade theologians as to the proper course to follow in cases where an apparent conflict appears between the historical reading of Scripture and a claim of natural science. Galileo's venture into the territory of the theologian almost certainly helped to precipitate the crisis that led to the banning of Copernicus's work. But John Paul II is kinder to its argument than were the theologians of that earlier day: "Galileo introduced a principle of interpretation of the sacred books which goes beyond the literal sense but conforms with the intention and the type of exposition proper to each book.... The Church's teaching authority admits the plurality of the modes of interpretation of Holy Scripture. The presence of different literary genres in the sacred books and therefore the necessity of discovering the mode of interpretation proper to each is taught expressly in the encyclical *Divino afflante Spiritu* of Pius XII." And so the hermeneutic principle espoused by Galileo, which seemed so alarming to Bellarmine and the Roman theologians of 1616, has now become part of the official teaching of the Church.

In the wake of John Paul's call for a deeper study of the Galileo affair, a Commission consisting of four study groups was set up in July 1982; the groups represented science and epistemology, exegesis, history, and culture respectively. Though there had been talk of some sort of juridical rehabilitation of Galileo, the Pope evidently decided that the best way to make amends for the Church's role in that unhappy episode was to encourage the fullest freedom in exploring the entire affair, and to draw attention to the fact that the Church now admits that the Biblical literalism on which the decree

vi

of 1616 rested is theologically inadequate.

John Paul alluded to Galileo again more recently during an official visit to Pisa, Galileo's birthplace. In a talk devoted mainly to the moral uses and abuses of scientific advances, delivered on September 22, 1989, he remarked: "How could we not remember the name of the great personage who was born here, and who took here his first steps towards a reputation that will never die." Galileo's scientific work, "imprudently opposed at the beginning, is now recognized by all as an essential stage in the methodology of research and, in general, on the road to the understanding of the natural world." The "imprudence" of the church's representatives in their opposition to Galileo's cosmological claims is officially acknowledged. But this still leaves open a tangle of questions that scholars continue to debate.

In line with the Pope's desire to broaden and deepen the study of the Galileo affair, the study group of the Galileo Commission dealing with matters of science and epistemology has commissioned a number of studies that have been published in a special series, *Studi Galileiani*, from the Vatican Observatory. The present volume is the fifth in this series, and is the second book-length contribution.

*   *   *   *   *   *   *   *   *

It was not surprising that the distinguished historian of science, Richard S. Westfall, should eventually turn his skills to the unravelling of the Galileo story. It is at the confluence, after all, of his two main interests, the historical relations of religion and science, and the development of the science of mechanics in the seventeenth century. His first book, *Religion and Science in Seventeenth Century England* (1958), traced the complex interactions between religious beliefs and the new science in that critical time and place, seventeenth century England. His second book, *Force in Newton's Physics* (1971), provided a detailed analysis of the conceptual structure of Newton's mechanics, drawing on a wealth of unpublished materials. His third major work was the magisterial *Never At Rest* (1980), an intellectual biography of Newton that is likely to remain the standard in Newton scholarship for many years to come. The lengthy chapter (entitled "Rebellion") on Newton's extensive theological writings is a major contribution in its own right. These writings lay unread, their existence barely known, until only a few decades ago; they remain for the most part unpublished still. Thanks to Dr. Westfall's labors, we now know a good deal more of Newton's twin theological passions: the interpretation of Biblical prophecy in precise numerical terms, and the pursuit of evidence to show that the Christian Church had lapsed into error in the fourth century by avowing the divinity of Christ.

In the last few years, Dr. Westfall has turned his attention as a historian to an intriguing feature of seventeenth century science, its dependence on patronage. Not many of those whose work would in later ages be recognized as the makers of an intellectual revolution could support themselves, as Robert Boyle did, by their own inherited means. The universities were, on the whole, unsympathetic to the new ideas. The day was still a long way off when industry and government would see in science a practical means of furthering their own goals. How, then, *were* the pioneers of the new science supported? Many sought out the patronage of the wealthy and powerful, on the understanding that their achievements would redound to the glory of discoverer and patron alike. It was an institution peculiarly of its time. And like all such, it holds a special fascination for the historian.

Of all those who sought the support of patrons for the furtherance of their own work, none was more successful than Galileo, successful both in the sense of attracting generous patronage and in rewarding his patrons with the glory he had promised them. Westfall argues that the quest for patronage shaped Galileo's career in ways that must be understood in order to grasp what happened in Rome and Florence in those tumultuous years. Making skilled use of the documents that have come down to us, particularly Galileo's own correspondence, he brings to life the events of that distant time in an interpretation that is always coherent and sometimes novel. He argues, for example, that the publication in 1632 of the controversial *Dialogue*, against all the odds, reflected both Galileo's need to appear worthy of the support being given him and Urban's own vanity as a patron of the arts.

The second main theme of this collection of essays is very different. Where patronage affected the course of events in ways that obviously could have taken a quite different turn, there was, Westfall argues, a fundamental disagreement in world-view also operative, one that led almost inexorably to a confrontation. Bellarmine and Galileo both began from theological premises, but they were radically different ones. Bellarmine believed in the primacy of the Scriptures as a source of truth and the inerrancy of Church tradition as a means of interpreting the Scriptures. Galileo saw two books where Bellarmine saw only one, and he took it to be obvious that the senses and reason with which God has endowed us are the means by which the Book of Nature is to be understood. Westfall argues that Bellarmine was the main source of the opposition to Galileo's views that manifested itself in Rome in 1615 and that led to the decree of 1616 that would later form the basis of the trial of 1633.

Other historians have regarded Bellarmine as relatively well-disposed to Galileo and as critical of Copernicanism on the grounds, in part, that no convincing proof had as yet been advanced in its favor. But Westfall believes that Bellarmine's earlier career and the tenor of his theological writings justify a different and less eirenic interpretation.

Pietro Redondi, in a widely-discussed recent book, *Galileo Heretic* (1983), argues that the real source of conflict between Galileo and the Church was not the Copernican doctrine, as everyone for centuries has supposed and as the documents seem to attest, but a suspicion of heresy in regard to Eucharistic doctrine. Galileo, like many other natural philosophers of his day, took atomism for granted and made occasional use of it in his theorizing. There was a real doubt on the part of some theologians, however, as to whether atomism could be squared with the doctrine of transubstantiation defined by the Council of Trent. Redondi noticed an unsigned denunciation of Galileo's atomism in the files of the Holy Office; starting from this rather slender clue, he constructed an ingenious and highly readable account of what might *really* have been going on in 1633.

Westfall is more sympathetic to the sheer imaginative achievement of Redondi's book than most historians have been. But he goes on to show, in a cumulative argument of impressive strength, just why the Redondi thesis will not wash. It is Westfall at his best, all of the documents open in his mind to the relevant passages, presenting us with an argument that can scarcely fail to convince.

This is the quality of scholarship that the exceptional complexities of the Galileo affair require. The working group on science and epistemology of the Galileo Commission will continue to encourage it in every way possible.

Ernan Mc Mullin
University of Notre Dame

1. The text of the Pope's address is printed as an Epilogue in *Galileo Galilei: Toward a Resolution of 350 Years of Debate, 1633-1683*, ed. Paul Cardinal Poupard, Pittsburgh: Duquesne University Press, 1987.

PREFACE

The four articles brought together in this fascicle of the *Studi Galileiani* of the Vatican Observatory were written on separate occasions over a period of about five years. I have made some minor alterations in order to eliminate repetitions among them, but I have not undertaken any fundamental revisions. Despite the fact that they were composed as independent publications, they appear to me to maintain a consistent outlook on Galileo, and I remain willing to stand by what I have said.

I wish to thank the Rev. George V. Coyne, S.J., of the Vatican Observatory and the Rev. Ernan McMullin of the University of Notre Dame, both of whom have helped to make this publication possible. Much of the research for the four papers was made possible by research grants from the National Science Foundation and the National Endowment for the Humanities and by a fellowship from the John Simon Guggenheim Memorial Foundation. I gratefully acknowledge their assistance.

"Bellarmino, Galileo, and the Clash of Two World Views" was published (under the title "The Trial of Galileo: Bellarmino, Galileo, and the Clash of Two Worlds") in *Journal for the History of Astronomy* (Science History Publications Ltd.), *20* (1989), 1 - 23. "Galileo and the Jesuits" appeared in R. S. Woolhouse, ed., *Metaphysics and Philosophy of Science in the Seventeenth and Eighteenth Centuries*, (Dordrecht: Kluwer Academic Publishers, 1988), pp. 45 - 72. A reduced version of "Patronage and the Publication of the *Dialogue*," was published in *History and Technology* (Harwood Academic Publishers GmbH), *4* (1987), 385 - 99. "*Galileo Heretic*: Problems, as they appear to me, with Redondi's thesis," appeared originally in *History of Science* (Science History Publications Ltd.), *26* (1988), 399 - 415. In all cases the publishers have graciously given permission for their reproduction here.

BELLARMINO, GALILEO, AND THE CLASH

OF TWO WORLD VIEWS

And because it has also come to the attention of the aforementioned Sacred Congregation [the final paragraph of a decree of 5 March 1616 by the Congregation of the Index stated] that the Pythagorean doctrine concerning the mobility of the earth and the immobility of the sun, which Nicholas Copernicus, *De revolutionibus orbium coelestium*, and Diego de Zùñiga [in his commentary] on Job also taught, and which is false and altogether incompatible with divine Scripture, is now spread abroad and accepted by many, as appears from a certain printed Epistle of a certain Carmelite Father [Foscarini] . . . ; therefore, in order that an opinion ruinous to Catholic truth not creep [*serpat*] further in this manner, the Sacred Congregation decrees that the said Nicholas Copernicus, *De revolutionibus orbium*, and Diego de Zùñiga on Job be suspended until corrected; that the book of the Carmelite Father Paolo Antonio Foscarini be indeed altogether prohibited and damned; and that all other books similarly teaching the same thing be prohibited: as accordingly it prohibits, damns, and suspends them all by the present Decree.[1]

Although Galileo was not mentioned in the decree of the Congregation of the Index, which made Copernican astronomy a forbidden topic among faithful Catholics for the following two centuries, the decree was the direct outcome of events of the previous two years that had centered on him. The decree was equally the direct outcome of the resolution Cardinal Roberto Bellarmino had begun to form almost as soon as Galileo had published his *Sidereus nuncius* early in 1610. The trial of Galileo in 1633, one of the climactic events of the Scientific Revolution, and indeed of all European history, would have been unthinkable without the prior decree of 1616, the culmination of what is sometimes called the first trial of Galileo. Central to both trials was the confrontation between two antithetical world views, embodied of course in Galileo and Bellarmino.

Galileo

In the case of Galileo as well as Bellarmino it is perhaps more valid to look back, not just to the previous two years, but beyond them to the *Sidereus nuncius*. Although there is evidence that Galileo may have considered himself a Copernican by 1597,[2] it took the telescopic discoveries to turn him into Copernicus' ardent champion. For other reasons as well, the *Sidereus nuncius*, the small book that announced the first discoveries, had made Galileo a figure of controversy. By naming the satellites of Jupiter after the ruling family in his native Tuscany and dedicating the book to Cosimo II, Galileo had used his discoveries to win appointment as Mathematician and Philosopher to the Grand Duke, and the handsome stipend that accompanied the appointment focused envy on him from the day he arrived home in Florence. Galileo was supremely self-assured and abrasively self-assertive in any case; the favor shown him by the Grand Duke did nothing to dull the cutting edge of his personality. Already in 1611, his friend Cigoli reported a rumor that Galileo's enemies around the Tuscan court were plotting to attack him through the Church on the issue of the motion of the earth,[3] and a year later Galileo confronted one of the leaders in the circle of his opponents, Niccolo Lorini, about statements he was reported to have made against Galileo.[4] It was not until 12 December 1613, however, that the rumors took on solid substance. On that day, Benedetto Castelli, Galileo's student, follower, and devoted friend, whom the master's influence had recently installed as Professor of Mathematics at the University of Pisa, was honored to dine with the court, then in residence in Pisa. Talk at dinner had centered on Galileo's discoveries, and one Cosimo Boscaglia, the Professor of Philosophy, had whispered in the ear of the dowager Grand Duchess, Christina of Lorraine, that passages in Scripture opposed the concept of a moving earth. As Castelli was leaving after dinner, he found himself called back to a further discussion, which lasted two hours, of Copernicanism and the Scriptures, in which everyone present understood that Castelli was substituting for Galileo, while the Grand Duchess actively attacked his position.[5]

In response to Castelli's report of this occasion, Galileo composed a long letter on the authority of Scripture in science.[6] For a year nothing further happened, at least overtly, though copies of Galileo's letter circulated in Florence. Then in December of 1614 a young Dominican anxious to make a name for himself, Tommaso Caccini, was preaching in Santa Maria Novella on the book of Joshua. When he came to the famous verse in which Joshua, needing more time to smite the Amorites, prayed that the sun should stand still, a passage which Galileo had explicated at length in his letter, Caccini suddenly launched into a vigorous attack on Galileo, Copernican astronomers, and mathematicians in general.[7] Caccini later testified before the Inquisition that Niccolo Lorini had shown him Galileo's letter to Castelli after the sermon.[8]   In view of the prominence of the passage in Joshua in Galileo's letter, this order of events is scarcely credible; on the contrary, one perceives the figure of Lorini lurking in the background from the beginning, busily stirring up the entire imbroglio. In any case, Caccini proceeded to lay a copy of Galileo's letter before the Inquisition in Florence, and when nothing happened, Lorini summoned up enough courage to make one move for himself and to send a copy of Galileo's letter to the Inquisition in Rome early in February 1615.

The Roman Inquisition was more vigorous than its Florentine office; it immediately initiated an investigation of Galileo, with the interrogation of witnesses and later the examination of one of his publications, which continued through the rest of 1615.[9]   In December Galileo, who understood that the charges against him were nearing their resolution, came to Rome to defend himself. At this point the record becomes confusing; one of my purposes in this paper is to offer a possible resolution, necessarily speculative in view of the evidence available, of the confusion. On the one hand, early in February, 1616, Galileo was writing home that he had cleared himself and convinced the authorities of his integrity.[10]   The silence of the Congregation of the Index on Galileo, together with absence of a condemnation by the Holy Office, certainly seems to indicate that he was not mistaken. The confusion arises from the fact that, on the other hand, scarcely two weeks after Galileo said he had cleared himself, the Holy Office asked its consultors to consider two propositions, that the sun is motionless in the center of the world, and that the earth moves in an orbit around the center and rotates on its axis.[11] Identified as "the propositions of the Mathematician Galileo," the two assertions were found to be heretical because opposed to passages in Scripture. That decision was the foundation of a private warning by the Holy Office to Galileo that he should abandon Copernicanism and of the decree by the Congregation of the Index that I have quoted. Why then was Galileo left untouched in public? Integrity in upholding opinions deemed heretical was not usually considered a virtue.

Bellarmino

Cardinal Bellarmino was undoubtedly an important factor, and probably the determinative agent, in the decision of the Church against the heliocentric system in 1616. Elevated to the dignity of cardinal by Clement VIII because, as the Pope said, "he has not his equal for learning in the Church of God,"[12] Bellarmino exercised a spiritual hegemony in Rome, because of his personal qualities, similar to his intellectual one. Nothing illustrates his position in the Church better than the scenes, incredible to the 20th century, at his death and funeral. Everyone recognized his saintliness; everyone was convinced that sainthood, in the Catholic definition of the term, would crown his life, as indeed it did finally, three centuries later. While Bellarmino lay dying, interminably it must have seemed, and in fact for two and a half weeks, cardinals and other prelates of the Church, worldly men who had not hesitated to exploit their positions to enrich themselves, testified by their actions that they nevertheless still acknowledged the medieval ideal of sainthood. Crowding into his chamber, touching and kissing his body, catching his blood in their handkerchiefs when leeches were applied to him, they refused to let the poor man die in peace. When death finally delivered him, they plundered his spartan quarters for relics, even ripping the clothes off his body -- indeed more than once. As he lay in state in the church of the Gesu, the mob -- not cardinals in this case, though one doubts that they would have held back at the end -- nearly tore the body apart for the same purpose, and only with difficulty did the authorities preserve his remains intact for burial.[13] Alive, he had been a member of every congregation of the cardinals in Rome. Cardinal del Monte left testimony that the Congregation of Rites, which included some thirteen other cardinals, often altered decisions reached by common consent of the others, because Bellarmino alone took the opposing side.[14] During the final years of his life, the Cardinal was prefect of both the Holy Office and the Congregation of the Index. This was after the events of 1615-16, to be sure, but he was very much a member of both at the time of those events and therefore, almost by definition, the most important voice in their decisions.[15]

     Roberto Bellarmino's whole existence had been shaped by the struggle against heresy. Born in 1542, he entered the world almost simultaneously with the outbreak of the initial war of religion (1546) and the founding of the Jesuit order (1540), the weapon of the Catholic Church against the Protestant heresy, in the service of which Bellarmino would spend his life. His years of childhood and education almost coincided with the Council of Trent (1545-63). Having entered the Society of Jesus in 1560, Bellarmino received his first important assignment at Louvain, in what is now Belgium, in 1569. The low countries were at that time the focal point of the struggle between Catholicism and Protestantism. Bellarmino's seven years in Louvain did much to determine the rest of his career. There he began the study of Protestant theology, his knowledge of which, unrivalled in the Catholic world, was the necessary foundation for his work of refutation.[16] There he met a band of English Catholics led by Nicholas Sanders, whose series of answers to the Protestant enemies appealed to Bellarmino's soul as precisely the sort of militant theology, girded for battle and facing the foe, that the age demanded.[17] Called back to the Society's *Collegio Romano* in 1576, he became the Professor of Controversial Theology in the most important university of the Jesuit order and indeed of the whole Catholic world. By their power, his great *Disputationes de controveriis christianae fidei, adversus nostri temporis haereticos*, in effect, the texts of his lectures delivered during the following twelve years in Rome, made Bellarmino the Catholic theologian most hated in Protestant Europe; they have demonstrated the solidity of their content by remaining the definitive statement of the principles of Catholic faith against the challenge of Protestantism down to our own age. Bellarmino experienced the battle not only as the clash of ideas but also as the clash of swords, and not merely from the safe distance of Rome. In 1590 he accompanied Cardinal Cajetan on his mission to France and was penned up with the Cardinal in Paris during the terrible blockade.[18]

Nor was Protestantism the only heresy the champion of the Catholic Church confronted as the entire edifice of the medieval world was beginning to crumble in the late years of the 16th century. New philosophies also challenged Catholic truth. In 1592, the Inquisition in Venice arrested Giordano Bruno after he had been incautious enough to venture back across the Alps, and a year later Venice had handed Bruno over to Rome. It does not appear to be true that Bellarmino was the principal factor in the ultimate condemnation and execution of Bruno, but there is no doubt that he participated prominently in the process. In 1599, after the Roman Inquisition had shown itself uncertain what to do with its prisoner and had merely left him to languish in prison, Bellarmino, with his years of confronting and defining error and his scholastic habit of reducing every issue to a numbered series of points, boiled the case against Bruno down to eight specific charges.[19] The horrific climax did not then wait much longer. At much the same time, quite another issue also associated with the collapse of the unified order of medieval Europe arose. Like other states of Europe, the Republic of Venice was determined to control the Church within its borders. In 1606 the Pope excommunicated the Doge and the Senate and laid the entire city under interdict until the republic repealed certain laws concerning ecclesiastical affairs and handed over to the Church two priests imprisoned in Venice. It was Bellarmino to whom the Catholic Church entrusted the task of replying to the pamphlets of Paolo Sarpi, the defender of Venetian claims.[20]   Soon thereafter James I of England raised much the same question, with all of the details altered, in his theory of the divine right of kings. Again it was Bellarmino who replied to James in the name of the Church.[21]

Not surprisingly, Roberto Bellarmino held definite views about truth and falsehood, and whatever the issue under discussion, he tended to express himself in those terms, usually unqualified by modifiers suggesting uncertainty or doubt.[22] Late in 1591 the Hungarian Jesuit, Stephen Arator, raised objections to passages in Bellarmino's *Controversies*. Replying with spirit, Bellarmino informed Aquaviva, the General of the order, about Arator, whose opinions he found "dangerous and in some cases embarrassing to the Company," "unacceptable and scandalous." Nor was that all; besides Arator's mistakes about the *Controversies*, Bellarmino found, he informed Aquaviva, more than ten erroneous doctrines in his statement; "and if I were not certain that you will remedy this by making him retract, and that he is prone to obey, I would feel obliged in conscience to denounce him to the Holy Office as a man who is dangerous in this time and in those places."[23] Some might think that heresy is a minor problem, he asserted in the preface of his *Controversies*.

> Let me say this one thing; the perversity of heretics is as much worse
> than all other evils and afflictions as the dreadful and fearful plague
> is worse than the more common diseases.[24]

Using the same figure years later, he congratulated Maximilian of Bavaria for keeping his lands free from "the dreadful contagion of false doctrine . . ."[25] On the whole, however, Bellarmino found military metaphors more expressive. He was, after all, a Jesuit. In his view of human history, the never ending struggle against heresy was the central theme. The "enemy of the human race" had not assaulted the truth of the Catholic Church without a plan, he argued, in a passage that sounds almost Manichean. During the first two centuries of the Christian era, he had concentrated on the first article of the creed, the conception of one God. When those heresies had failed, he turned during the third and fourth centuries against the second article, the nature of Christ, and then to the mystery of the incarnation and to the doctrine of the Holy Spirit. Failing also in all these attempts, he began about the year 1000 to attack the articles of the creed that concern the Church and the sacraments, and that battle still raged. Bellarmino referred to "the most crafty enemy" who continually schemes against us, and no one is likely to object when I assert that he saw himself called upon to lead the Church in the ongoing war against the foe of humanity itself.[26]

Of necessity, from the nature of the controversies in which he engaged, Bellarmino had a carefully elaborated conception of divine revelation and its authority. Against the Catholic Church, Protestantism had raised the standard of Scripture as the sole authority in matters of faith. Bellarmino replied to the Protestants by insisting that Catholics revered the word of God every bit as much as they did. He devoted the first "Controversy" in his great work to "The Word of God," and he began his exposition with a demonstration that "the Prophetic & Apostolic books . . . are the true word of God, & the certain and fixed rule of faith."[27] However, Bellarmino continued, distinguishing himself from Protestant bibliolators with precision, Scripture is not so open in itself that without explication it is sufficient to settle all controversies about the faith. The manifold differences of interpretation among Protestants seemed to demonstrate this proposition without further argument. Frequently passages in Scripture have two senses, a literal one and a spiritual or mystical one. Thus the flight from Egypt, the crossing of the Red Sea, and the manna that fed Israel all have, in addition to their literal meaning, a spiritual meaning for Christians. Moreover, the literal meaning can be twofold -- simple (which is the direct meaning of the words) and figurative (by which the words take on a different meaning). When Christ says, in John x, that he has other sheep which are not of this fold, he means, in a literal but figurative sense, other men beyond the Jews. A literal sense is found in every sentence in both the Old and the New Testaments, and occasionally there are several literal meanings in the same sentence. Although spiritual meanings are common, every sentence does not have one of them. The command to love the Lord with all your heart has only the one, literal meaning. Nothing in Bellarmino's analysis corresponded precisely to the problem Galileo would raise about passages expressed in the language of the common people. However, the notion was not original with Galileo by any means, and Bellarmino would certainly have agreed that one cannot accept the simple literal meaning of anthropomorphic statements attributing human limbs and human passions to God. His doctrine of interpretation seems so readily adaptable to this small extension that there is no need to pause with it. "This in general we say:" Bellarmino concluded, "the judge of the true sense of Scripture and of all controversies is the Church, that is, the Pope with a Council in which all Catholics come together."[28]

Since Bellarmino's insistence, that is, the orthodox Catholic insistence, on the Church would later bear directly on Galileo, let us pause with it for a moment. His concept of the word of God included an unwritten word of God. This did not refer, as it would for Galileo and numerous other scientists of the 17th century, to nature as the creation of God. It referred rather to the tradition of the Church. The Scriptures without tradition are neither necessary nor sufficient. They are not necessary because tradition alone preserved the Church before the time of Moses, though Bellarmino conceded that in this latter corrupted age the Scriptures are necessary. They are not sufficient, however. Some authority must establish what is the true revelation of God. Moreover, the Scriptures are often ambiguous and perplexed and cannot be understood unless interpreted by an authority which cannot err. That authority, of course, is the Church that embodies the authentic tradition. "For the universal Church not only cannot err in believing," Bellarmino asserted, "but also not in acting and especially in rites and divine worship . . ." When all of the learned teachers [*doctores*] agree on something, then it must be true. "The reason . . . is that if all the learned Teachers of the Church can err when they agree on some opinion, then the whole Church errs . . ."[29] Why can the whole Church not err? Because it is not an institution of men but an institution of God, an institution founded by God, an institution ruled by God. When Bellarmino wrote the words above about the inability of all the learned teachers of the Church to err, he was defending the Catholic tradition against Protestant attack. As Galileo would find out on a wholly different issue, Bellarmino did not limit the scope of that judgment to traditions challenged by Protestantism.

In Bellarmino's view, the role of the Church as the ordained interpreter did not derogate from the authority of Scripture but rather enhanced it. "Scripture," he insisted, "is the word of God immediately revealed & written in a certain way as God speaks. . . . The sacred writers are said to have had an immediate revelation, & to have written the words of God himself, because either certain new & hitherto unknown things were revealed to them by God . . . Or God immediately inspired, & moved the writers to write what they saw or heard, & guided them so that they did not err in any way." He went on to add that "in Scripture there can be no error whether it is concerned with faith or with morals, & whether something general & common to the whole Church is asserted, or something particular, & pertaining only to one man. . . . in Scripture not only the sentences but also each & every word pertains to faith. Indeed we believe that no word has been used in Scripture at random or incorrectly."[30]

Although Bellarmino, who found in the defense of Catholicism in those strenuous times work enough to fill a hundred lives, never devoted himself primarily to natural philosophy, he did have occasion to touch on topics of astronomy when first he lectured at Louvain in the period 1570-72.   Already at that time, on matters not directly concerned with Copernicanism and forty years before Galileo would prompt a confrontation with the heliocentric system, Bellarmino was projecting the literal word of the Bible into questions of astronomy in a way that sounds surprisingly like Protestant fundamentalism in a later age on a different issue.   One must resist any temptation to apply the word "arrogant" to Bellarmino.   A prince of the Church who was ready to take his turn in the scullery at the *Collegio Romano*, he made his whole life an implicit protest against the arrogance all too common among contemporary members of the hierarchy of the Church he served.   Nevertheless, Bellarmino never doubted that he had recognized that one thing of great value, and he never doubted that everything else was to be measured by its standard. A sense, which one might mistakenly confuse with arrogance, that he represented the spiritual elite pervades his autobiography.   Technical astronomy was not one of the primary concerns of the spiritual elite; with all eternity stretching before him, Bellarmino could not understand why some men thought that the physical structure of the universe was so important. Baldini and Coyne have emphasized how Bellarmino's biblicism freed him to recognize the hypothetical nature of much contemporary astronomy and thus to question it.   One should add to this that the basis on which he questioned contemporary astronomy was not astronomical evidence but Scripture.

How many heavens are there?   Bellarmino answered three, while noting that some "stupid astrologers [read astronomers]" claimed there are as many heavens as there are heavenly bodies.   Because the Hebrew word *shamayim* has only the plural form, its use in Scripture does not allow us to settle whether there is a single heaven or more than one. However, the Scriptures definitely refer in other language to two heavens and apparently to a third, and almost all of the Church fathers can be brought into conformity with the latter number.[31]   Are the sun and the stars fixed in the sky so that they move with its motion?   Scripture does not say they are; its implication is quite the opposite, that they move independently in the sky like birds in the air and fish in the sea. Bellarmino went on to note that philosophers were not in agreement about the motions of the heavenly bodies and that it was not the business of theologians to consider the technical arguments of different hypotheses. "Thus it is possible for us to select among them the one which best corresponds to the Sacred Scriptures."[32]   As Bellarmino understood this statement, he was not selecting the hypothesis most congenial to theologians, but, without reference to astronomical evidence, the one which was true.   Was the moon, next to the sun, the largest body in the heavens? Despite the fact that astronomers, as he knew, made the moon the smallest celestial body except for Mercury, Bellarmino was convinced that it ranked with the sun because the Scriptures referred to those two as "luminaria magna."[33]

Years later, indeed exactly one year after the Church's judgment against Copernicanism, Bellarmino returned to the question of the size of the moon. Do not object to me that astronomers disagree, he said. They cannot demonstrate their opinion, and the Scriptures speak of the two great luminaries. "Besides did not St. Augustine (*De Genesi ad litteram* xxi, 16) say that it is much better to believe the scriptures than the astrologers with respect to the size of the moon . . . ?"[34] Bellarmino concluded the latter passage with the statement that he had never wanted to enter into hostilities with astronomers. But one must understand that, for all the intended charity of his gesture, it assumed that astronomers would recognize their place, as theologians such as Bellarmino defined it, and that they would stay there.

This was the man who witnessed, along with everyone else in Europe and especially in Italy, the display of celestial fireworks that Galileo orchestrated in 1610. It is worth recalling that only a decade earlier he had been involved deeply in the traumatic trial of Giordano Bruno. Although it is often asserted that the Church pursued Bruno and burned him at the stake because he held Copernican beliefs, this is flatly untrue. The principal charges against Bruno were theological by any reasonable definition of the word -- related to issues such as transubstantiation, the Trinity, and the substantiality of the individual soul. However, matters concerned with natural philosophy had been involved in the proceedings against Bruno from the beginning, and they also appeared in Bellarmino's list of eight charges. Prominent among them was the doctrine of the plurality of worlds, which is not explicitly Copernican but which had a historical affinity with Copernicanism.[35] Although the motion of the earth was not listed as a charge against Bruno, interrogations did raise the question and treat it as repugnant to the faith.[36] It would not be surprising, against this background, if the *Sidereus nuncius*, an explicitly Copernican book, aroused the suspicions of a man accustomed to believe that eternal truth was eternally under attack.

The Developing Conflict

Although the *Sidereus nuncius* was unmistakable in its adhesion to heliocentric astronomy, it apparently took the later observation of the phases of Venus, in December 1610, to turn Galileo into Copernicus' crusading champion. No sooner did he discover the phases of Venus than Galileo arranged a trip to Rome, where he began openly to assume the role of advocate. He arrived in the Papal city on 29 March 1611 and found himself immediately an object of attention. Federico Cesi gave a magnificent banquet in his honor and inducted him into his *Accademia dei Lincei*. In May the *Collegio Romano* arranged a convocation in his honor. Well before the convocation he had met Cardinal Bellarmino and helped him to observe the new celestial phenomena that the telescope revealed.[37] The Cardinal cannot have failed to note the confidence with which Galileo proclaimed the demise of the geocentric system. I assume it was after this encounter when Bellarmino wrote to Father Clavius and his mathematical colleagues in the *Collegio Romano* on 19 April, asking whether Galileo's five major observations -- the multitude of stars invisible to the naked eye, Saturn's strange shape, the phases of Venus, the roughness of the lunar surface, and the satellites of Jupiter -- were "well-founded" or whether they might not be "a mere illusion." While offering minor differences of interpretation in two cases, the Jesuit astronomers assured Bellarmino that the observations were indeed well founded.[38] Nevertheless, a month later, on 17 May, shortly after the convocation in the *Collegio Romano*, the Holy Office entered the first reference to Galileo into its minutes.

Let it be seen whether Galileo, a Professor of Philosophy and Mathematics, is named in the case of Doct. Cesare Cremonini.[39]

Cremonini, a prominent Aristotelian philosopher at Padua, where he had been at once the friend and opponent of Galileo, was under almost continual investigation by the Inquisition from 1604 until his death because of the naturalism of his philosophy. Needless to say, the record does not specify who raised the query. Nevertheless, Bellarmino was one of seven cardinals of the congregation present that day, and when all things are considered -- his role in combatting heresy, his familiarity with Venetian developments, his ascendancy in the Holy Office, his enquiry to the *Collegio Romano* about Galileo's discoveries, and later events yet to be mentioned -- it is difficult to believe that he was not the source of the question.

A year later Galileo was preparing his letters on sunspots, which insisted against Scheiner, who strove to preserve the immutability of the heavens, on the evidence the sunspots offered of corruption and change.

Near the beginning of July, 1612, along with a copy of his recently published *Discourse on Bodies in Water*, Galileo addressed a letter to Cardinal Conti, prefect of the Congregation of the Index, asking about the extent to which Scripture seemed to dictate certain aspects of Aristotelian philosophy. Conti replied that Scripture says nothing about the incorruptibility of the heavens and the orbital motion of the earth; it does state unequivocally that heavenly bodies rise and set, though it could be speaking the language of the common people in these passages. Apparently still not satisfied, Galileo wrote again and received another answer to the same effect.[40] The second letter on sunspots, which Galileo dated 14 August, after Conti's initial letter though before his following one, proceeded then to conclude its extended argument for the mutability of the heavens with the assertion that this opinion was also conformable "to the indubitable truths of the Holy Scriptures which in many places that are very clear and obvious assert the unstable and fallen nature of the heavenly matter."[41] Toward the end of the year, however, when Prince Cesi sought to gain a license for the *Letters* which his *Accademia dei Lincei* was publishing, the censors suddenly began to find problems with the reference to Scripture, and the book could not appear until Galileo had removed it.[42] Again no specific name appeared, only "the censors." Nevertheless one begins to get the impression of a watchful presence monitoring a potential source of dangerous ideas.

Galileo's *Letters on Sunspots*, a more blatantly Copernican book than the *Sidereus nuncius*, appeared in the spring of 1613. There followed that December the dinner with the Grand Ducal family in Pisa and a year later Caccini's sermon in Florence and the denunciation to the Inquisition, as I have already related. It is perhaps relevant to the argument to note that Lorini and his friends, in sending Galileo's letter to Castelli to Rome, were explicit in their desire that Cardinal Bellarmino see it.[43] Even before the denunciation, however, a Galileo greatly agitated by Caccini's sermon wrote to Cesi at the end of December. It seems to me that the import of Cesi's reply in January has not been sufficiently noted. Cesi wrote from his country seat in Acquasparta, some eighty kilometers (to use a later unit of measure) north of Rome. He had left the papal city early in October, long before Caccini's sermon.[44] What he had to say about opinion in Rome was so phrased that it clearly implied oral communication rather than correspondence, and it appears to me that it must have reflected information he had received prior to and independent of the event in Florence. Cesi assured Galileo that he understood his feelings, but "with things as they are at the [Papal] Court," he urged him in the strongest terms to contain his resentment and to conduct himself "with great revelation; both the Bible and nature "proceed alike from the divine Word, the former as the dictate of the Holy Ghost and the latter as the observant executrix of God's commands."[48] The Bible speaks in the language of the common people, and in many places its literal meaning cannot be accepted. Thus the literal words of Scripture attribute feet, hands, and eyes to God and ascribe to him emotions such as anger, repentance, and hatred, passages which would, if accepted literally, lead one into "grave heresies and follies."[49] In contrast to the Bible in this respect, nature is "inexorable and immutable; she never transgresses the laws imposed upon her, or cares one whit whether her abstruse reasons and methods of operation are understandable to men."[50] Galileo insisted further, and this was the crux of his argument, "that two truths cannot contradict one another . . ."[51] It is then the function of expositors of the Bible to find the correct interpretation of Scripture, which must agree with the well-established conclusions of natural philosophy.

The purpose of Scripture is to persuade men to those doctrines necessary to their salvation. Galileo was adamant that science had nothing to say about doctrines of faith, and he acknowledged the inerrancy of Scripture on such matters. On the other hand, the Bible does not attempt to treat natural philosophy. For example, it hardly addresses astronomy, and does not so much as mention any of the planets.[52] If it was the intention of God to employ Revelation to instruct mankind in astronomy, surely He would have devoted more attention to it. Galileo could not believe, he continued, "that the same God who has endowed us with senses, reason, and intellect has intended to forego their use and by some other means to give us knowledge which we can attain by them."[53] Thus he concluded that "it would be the part of prudence not to permit anyone to usurp scriptural texts and force them in some way to maintain any physical conclusion to be true, when at some future time the senses and demonstrative or necessary reasons may show the contrary."[54]

His opponents were proceeding in an irregular manner. If they really believed that they had the correct sense of Scripture, it followed inevitably that they had "the absolute truth" on the issue under debate. Hence they had a great advantage. Because they advocated the truth, they had to have "many sense-experiences and rigorous proofs" on their side, while Galileo could have only illusory appearances, quibbles, and fallacies. Why then, with this advantage, did they seize instead "the dreadful weapon which cannot be turned aside . . . ?"[55] To conclude the letter Galileo offered a brilliant exposition of the famous passage from Joshua which Caccini would make the occasion of his attack. Caccini cannot have read very carefully, for Galileo demonstrated conclusively that caution."

> As for the theory of Copernicus [Cesi continued], Bellarmino himself, who is among the principal figures in the congregations concerned with these things, has told me that he considers it heretical, and that the motion of the earth is, beyond any doubt, contrary to Scripture: so that you can see how things stand. I have always wondered whether he would not, when he finds it convenient, bring Copernicus up in the Congregation of the Index and have him prohibited, nor is there need to say more.

Cesi went on to counsel Galileo to stand out of sight while others manned the defense, which should concentrate on Caccini's attack on mathematics and remain entirely silent about astronomy, and again he warned Galileo to "proceed cautiously."[45] It has been the almost universal opinion that Galileo's troubles with the Church began in Florence, with Lorini, Boscaglia, Caccini, and others of that circle. The implication of Cesi's letter, which I find unavoidable, however, is that prior to Caccini's sermon and independently of events in Florence Cardinal Bellarmino had decided that Copernican astronomy was opposed to Scriptural truth and would have to be suppressed. With its repeated warnings to Galileo, the letter also implies that Bellarmino had expressed some reservations about him as well. This puts the whole of the trial in a new perspective. As for the exchange between Galileo and Bellarmino during 1615, it is best understood if we realize that both men came to it with their minds made up.

The Exchange of 1615

Obviously, Galileo did not initially address the long letter about science and Scripture, written to Castelli in the wake of his report on the dinner in Pisa, to Bellarmino. When he heard that a copy of the letter had been sent to the Inquisition, however, he feared that it might have been altered in a way that would injure him, and he hastened to send a correct copy of the original to Rome. He was anxious that the Cardinal see it.[46] Galileo's enemies, in their desire to lay the matter before Bellarmino, appear to have understood the Cardinal better than he did. Meanwhile, we can legitimately treat the letter to Castelli as the first item in their exchange.

The Bible is the word of God, Galileo agreed; "the Holy Scriptures can never speak untruth or err . . ."[47] Interpreters of the Bible are human, however, and they can err. Nature, as the creation of God, is also His if the literal meaning of Scripture is the criterion, the passage in Joshua is incompatible with the Ptolemaic system.[56]

The letter to Castelli presented a powerful argument for the independence of science from theological domination. Bellarmino's insistence that Scripture is unable to err expressed one of Christianity's central affirmations, which animated the ideal for which he spoke -- that God has revealed himself to mankind. To Bellarmino and the Church this meant that truth in everything that matters is known, and that activities such as natural philosophy, which are subordinate to the ultimate end of mankind, must be carried on within the boundaries defined by revealed truth. The power of Galileo's letter to Castelli lay in his appeal to other equally central affirmations of the faith and in his ability to weave from them the fabric of the new ideal he represented -- that the world also proceeds from the word of God, and that God has created man in His own image. Bellarmino would have served his Church well had he been capable of imagining, after a lifetime spent defending the faith, that he was not the sole custodian of the ark.

Early in 1615 the Carmelite theologian, Paolo Foscarini, published a *Letter . . . on the Opinion of the Pythagoreans and of Copernicus concerning the Mobility of the Earth and the Stability of the Sun*, addressed to Sebastiano Fantoni, General of the Order of Carmelites.[57] Foscarini wrote as a Copernican, convinced that only the Copernican system was consistent with the new observations of the telescope, and concerned to refute the objection that heliocentric astronomy is impossible because it is repugnant to Scripture. Dated 6 January 1615, the letter appeared too early to have been a reply to Caccini's sermon; it thus offers further testimony that a number of people perceived independently that the Copernican issue was coming to a head about 1615 and that it was not solely the circle of Galileo's enemies in Florence who precipitated the crisis.

Foscarini's argument, that the Scriptures speak in the language of the common people, was very similar to Galileo's. For my purposes, the importance of the letter lies in the facts that its author requested Cardinal Bellarmino's opinion on it and that Bellarmino, by lumping Galileo together with Foscarini and by insuring that Galileo immediately saw a copy of his reply, effectively made it a commentary on the letter to Castelli.[58] First, Foscarini and Galileo would act prudently, Bellarmino began in his typically numbered sequence of points, by speaking only hypothetically and not absolutely. To say that celestial appearances are explained better on the Copernican supposition is to speak well, but to affirm that the sun is the center of the universe and that the earth moves "is a very dangerous attitude and one calculated not only to annoy all scholastic philosophers and theologians but also to injure our holy faith by contradicting the Scriptures." One might observe two points in passing: that the later actions of both the Holy Office and the Congregation of the Index condemned Copernicanism in terms of exactly these two propositions about the sun and the earth, and that Bellarmino, if not a scholastic philosopher, was most assuredly a scholastic theologian, and was thus proclaiming his own annoyance. He continued, second, that the Council of Trent had forbidden the interpretation of Scripture in a way contrary to the common opinion of the Fathers, but all of the Fathers agreed in interpreting the critical passages as saying that the sun is in the heavens and revolves around the earth which is at rest. "Consider then, in your prudence," he added, in what Galileo should have read as a warning couched in the gravest terms, "whether the Church can tolerate that the Scriptures should be interpreted in a manner contrary to that of the holy Fathers and of all modern commentators . . ." It would not do to say that this is not a matter of faith. He who denies that Abraham had two sons and Jacob twelve is as much a heretic as he who denies the virgin birth of Christ, "because it is the Holy Spirit who makes known both truths by the mouth of the Prophets and Apostles." Third, if there were a real proof of the Copernican system, we should have to proceed cautiously with the Scriptures and acknowledge that we do not comprehend them. But there is no such proof, and hence we should be very careful in abandoning the established interpretation. Solomon, who wrote that the sun rises and sets, was a man learned beyond all others in the knowledge of created things; he would not have spoken in contradiction to the truth.

Near the beginning of the twentieth century, Pierre Duhem pointed to Bellarmino's letter as a clearer expression of the scientific attitude than Galileo's. Naively overconfident in science, Galileo spoke as though the conclusions he defended were demonstrated truths, while Bellarmino, who had digested the medieval tradition of "saving the phenomena," understood correctly the hypothetical nature of Copernicanism.[59] This may all be well and good when we restrict ourselves only to parts of Bellarmino's letter, but if we are discussing science, we need to recall other parts of it, which were also essential aspects of Bellarmino's position -- to wit, that the word of Scripture, which speaks the truth of God, outweighs the hypothetical conclusions of science, not just in questions of theology, but also in questions of science.

We need also to recall the conclusion of the letter, which Duhem neglected to mention. Restricting himself there to scientific considerations, Bellarmino forgot what he had just said about hypotheses. In the final sentences he brought up the comparison with a man watching the shore from a moving ship, used by Copernicans to justify the assertion that celestial appearances will be the same whether the heavens turn from east to west once a day or the earth turns on its axis from west to east. The comparison is not valid, Bellarmino told Foscarini and Galileo, because a man on a ship knows very well that the shore is at rest, and he can correct the illusion. "But as to the sun and the earth a wise man has no need to correct his judgment, for his experience tells him plainly that the earth is standing still and that his eyes are not deceived when they report that the sun, moon, and stars are in motion." Less than a year later, when the consultors of the Holy Office were called upon to consider the two propositions about the stability of the sun and the motion of the earth, they did not confine themselves to a theological opinion. Both propositions they concluded, in words that might be mistaken for a summary of Bellarmino's letter, as they probably were, are not only heretical but absurd in philosophy.[60]

Galileo received Bellarmino's letter well before the end of April. As we know from his correspondence with Msgr. Dini, he was at that time expanding the letter to Castelli into the considerably longer *Letter to the Grand Duchess Christina*. An extended section of the new treatise addressed itself to "some theologians whom I consider men of profound learning and devout behavior" whom he held in great esteem.[61] Who can doubt that he had Bellarmino in mind? Indeed it appears to me that the entire revision of the letter to Castelli was addressed to Bellarmino. There is no evidence that Bellarmino saw it, but I find it difficult to believe that he did not. If Galileo had not succeeded in having the *Letter* delivered to the Cardinal before December, he would have brought a copy with him when he came to Rome. His letters from Rome to the court in Florence mentioned his efforts to present his case directly to the men who counted; There was no one in Rome who fitted that description better than Bellarmino.[62] It appears to me that we are unlikely to miss the mark in considering the *Letter to the Grand Duchess Christina* as part of the dialogue between the two men.

Since the *Letter to the Grand Duchess* embodied the letter to Castelli, much of it verbatim, there is no need to repeat its central argument. In the newly added address to some theologians of profound learning, Galileo confessed with candor that they [that is, Bellarmino] made him uncomfortable when they pretended, on scriptural authority, to constrain others, in physical matters, to follow opinions the theologians found in agreement with the Bible, but then believed themselves not bound to answer the opposing evidence and arguments. Theologians asserted that theology is queen of all the sciences. Galileo found an equivocation in the concept. If they meant that theology excels the others in dignity, he agreed, but theology is not queen in the sense that it contains the subordinate sciences and can therefore dictate their conclusions. To censure Copernicanism at that time, just as evidence that confirmed it was appearing, would give men an occasion "to see a proposition proved that it was heresy to believe." And to censure the whole science of astronomy would be to censure a hundred passages in the Bible that teach how the glory of God can be read in the book of the heavens.

> For let no one believe [Galileo spoke to Bellarmino here as one professional to another, insisting with the voice of the new world view on the dignity of scientific disciplines, almost pleading with Bellarmino to perceive that something had come to exist beyond the boundaries of his closed medieval universe] that reading the lofty concepts written in that book leads to nothing further than the mere seeing of the splendor of the sun and the stars and their rising and setting, which is as far as the eyes of brutes and of the vulgar can penetrate. Within its pages are couched mysteries so profound and concepts so sublime that the vigils, labors, and studies of hundreds upon hundreds of the most acute minds have still not pierced them even after continual investigations for thousands of years. . . . that which presents itself to mere sight is as nothing in comparison to the high marvels that the ingenuity of learned men discovers in the heavens by long and accurate observation.[63]

To Bellarmino's statement that there was no demonstration of the truth of the heliocentric system, Galileo replied in effect that the story of natural philosophy was only beginning to be told and that, whatever the conclusiveness of present demonstrations, theology would be wise if it refused to commit itself to the literal word of the Bible on questions subject in principle to confirmation by evidence of the senses or by necessary demonstrations. The man who only recently had discovered a host of new bodies and new truths in the sky, and who before that had elaborated the structure of what he would later publish as a "new science" of motion, was convinced that human knowledge, and especially knowledge of nature, increases over time. Already in the letter to Castelli, in a passage I have quoted, he referred to what the sciences might prove "at some future time." References to the possibility of further proofs at some later time pervade the *Letter to the Grand Duchess*. Duhem must have failed to notice them; in my opinion they seriously modify what he had to say about Galileo's scientific attitude. The Fathers of the Church, Galileo said, knew how prejudicial it would be to use Scripture to decide physical conclusions when experience and reason   "might in time"   show the contrary.[64]   Insisting on the literal text in questions of philosophy could prejudice the dignity of the Bible in the event that "later truth" showed the contrary.[65] To Bellarmino, in contrast, truth was known; the problem was not to expand it but to defend it against error. No more pronounced difference separated the two men. Especially here Galileo expressed the world view of the new age, calling in vain across the chasm that divided it from the one now passing away.

If he called here in vain, in other respects Galileo failed even more. He opened the *Letter* with an account of the envy his astronomical discoveries had created and the assertion that personal animosities against him were the source of the whole issue. This theme continued throughout the treatise. Bellarmino could examine himself, however, for evidence that more than personal motives were in play. With the assistance of Castelli, Galileo, who had probably never read a book by Augustine from beginning to end, filled the *Letter* with quotations from his works and from other Fathers of the Church. Bellarmino, a profound student of patristic literature, was bound to have recognized the shallowness of Galileo's knowledge in this respect, and one can readily imagine how gladly he received instruction on the Fathers from such a master. And Galileo could hardly have found a theme more likely to antagonize the man he addressed than his treatment of interpreters and interpretations of the Bible. To Bellarmino, the learned teachers of the Church, speaking in unanimity, expressed the truth of God. Galileo treated them as mere fallible human beings. He suggested to Bellarmino that the universal agreement of the Fathers should count only on those propositions which they had discussed carefully. The motion of the earth was not such a proposition; Galileo wondered if the question had ever entered their minds.[66] Thus he proceeded again to explain away the passage in Joshua as he had done before.

> As to other scriptural passages which seem to be contrary to this opinion [he continued], I have no doubt that if the opinion itself were known to be true and proven, those very theologians who, so long as they deem it false, hold these passages to be incapable of harmonious exposition with it, would find interpretations for them which would agree very well, and especially if they would add some knowledge of astronomical science to their knowledge of divinity.[67]

Galileo never ceased to be enamored of the brilliance of his own wit. In this case he was seeking to convince one of the very theologians he was choosing to lampoon, a man who saw himself as part of a tradition inspired by God. Whatever hair was left on Bellarmino's seventy year old head must have stood straight up when he read those words. As it happened, and as Galileo knew very well, the man thus satirized was also the dominant voice in the Holy Office.

As I said above, I find it impossible to believe that Bellarmino did not receive and read the *Letter to the Grand Duchess*. His reply to it was twofold, an equally eloquent composition of his own and a decisive official act. The composition was his great devotional tract, *De ascensione mentis in Deum, The Mind's Ascent to God*. In the literal sense, it is improper to treat *De ascensione* as a reply to the *Letter*. Although Bellarmino published it in 1615, the year of their exchange, he had composed it the previous autumn.[68] Nevertheless the tract, beyond its devotional purpose, which transcends its age, spoke so directly to the issues that Galileo had already injected into the age that one can legitimately consider *De ascensione* as the supreme expression of the medieval world view replying to the new age Galileo represented. We mortal men, Bellarmino asserted in his introduction, "find no other ladder whereby to ascend unto God, than the works of God." All creatures are the works of God; "man and the angels are not only his works, but also his images, as the Scriptures teach us."[69] If the words sound at first like those of Galileo, Bellarmino followed them down a path that diverged completely. Where for Galileo nature as the work of God demanded that we study its structure with faculties which are also divinely created, Bellarmino strove to raise his soul to God by learning from the world to despise it. The seventh step in the mind's ascent is the consideration of the heavens.

> But, my soul, rise thou up a little higher, if thou canst, and as thou observest the great splendour of the sun, the beauty of the moon, the number and variety of other luminaries, the wonderful harmony of the heavens and the delightful movement of the stars, consider: what it will be to see God above the heavens, as it were a sun, 'dwelling in the light which no man can approach unto' [1 Tim. vi, 16] . . . Thus it will come to pass that the beauty of the heavens will not appear so very great, and the things that are beneath the sky will seem altogether insignificant, indeed almost nothing, and to be considered despicable and worthy of contempt.[70]

If Galileo's *Letter* called in vain across the chasm dividing two worlds, so did Bellarmino's *Ascent* call just as vainly from the farther side. Like the passage above, it is filled with quotations from Scripture, which Bellarmino must have known by heart. That testimony in the language of the common people, which Galileo had to interpret away lest it impede the progress of science, was to Bellarmino, in its every word, a priceless guide to those things which alone matter in life. He had observed Galileo's self-esteem at first hand, and at times he seemed to speak directly to him, as a priest.

> Wherefore, my soul, if thou are wise, pursue the knowledge of salvation and the wisdom of the saints which lies in this, that thou fear God and keep his commandments: that prayer delight thee more than disputations, and the charity which buildeth up more than the knowledge which puffeth up; for this is the way that leadeth unto life and the kingdom of heaven . . .[71]

But Galileo was no more capable of comprehending Bellarmino's call than Bellarmino his. I have spoken of the clash of two world views. The clash occurs in our 20th century minds. Instead of clashing in the early 17th century, they passed by each other wholly without contact.

The Condemnation of 1616

On another plane, however, there was contact enough, for Bellarmino commanded the repressive machinery of the Church. The charge lodged against Galileo in February 1615 focused on the letter to Castelli, and the Inquisition's investigation concentrated initially on it. In fact they found there nothing of substance at all. Nevertheless someone kept the investigation alive. On 25 November, 1615, the Holy Office resolved to examine Galileo's *Letters on Sunspots*,[72] and in February 1616 it found two "propositions of the Mathematician Galileo" heretical and absurd in philosophy -- the same two propositions that Cardinal Bellarmino had found heretical and absurd in philosophy in his letter to Foscarini. As we have seen, however, the Holy Office did not condemn the author of the two propositions. We have good evidence that Galileo had his defenders in Rome. Maffeo Barberini would later claim that he had preserved him in 1616,[73] and there were in addition Galileo's other two patrons, the Grand Duke Cosimo de' Medici and Prince Federico Cesi of the *Accademia dei Lincei*. The general context, with Galileo's prominence on the intellectual scene, suggests that they were not the only defenders.

Can one explain the contradictions in the record of 1616 by assuming that a compromise was struck? Bellarmino had no personal vendetta to wage against Galileo. He was not a member of the Florentine League of Pigeons, who were apparently moved by envy as Galileo always claimed.[74] On the contrary, his concern was solely to preserve Catholic truth in his age from the unending assault of heresy. Can we assume then that he accepted a compromise? There would be no need to condemn Galileo if, on the one hand, the Congregation of the Index would move unambiguously against Copernicanism and if, on the other hand, the principal agent in the promotion of Copernicanism were solemnly ordered to desist. Let me be frank in labelling the assumption as speculation, which every interpretation of the trial inevitably becomes, given the evidence available. The speculative assumption appears to me to explain the known facts, however, and it does not completely lack supportive evidence. There is at least one indication in the wording of the decree by the Congregation of the Index that Bellarmino himself composed it.[75] There is more than an indication of his participation in the order to Galileo. Of the various other prelates available for the task, it was nevertheless busy Cardinal Bellarmino whom, at the meeting of the Holy Office, His Holiness instructed -- at Bellarmino's own insistence, I am suggesting -- to call Galileo in and warn him to abandon the condemned opinion. Busy Cardinal Bellarmino found time to carry out the commission the very next day.[76]

The record of the interview in which Bellarmino issued the warning has been the subject of controversy since it became known about a hundred years ago. The document is not properly signed, and what it registers is not in agreement with the instructions given by the Holy Office. Bellarmino was to warn Galileo to give up the condemned opinion, and if Galileo refused to obey, the Commissary General of the Holy Office was to order him before witnesses and a notary to abstain altogether from teaching and defending a doctrine of this sort and from treating it. The document states that Galileo acquiesced and promised to obey, but it nevertheless indicates that (in what was supposed to follow if he refused to obey) Galileo was ordered to relinquish the opinion altogether and not to hold, teach, or defend it in any way, orally or in writing. Commentary has frequently assumed that gentle compassionate Saint Roberto would not have done anything harsh.[77] But gentle compassionate Saint Roberto had a backbone of steel. He held stern notions about the "divine wrath of God" and "how great must be his hatred of crimes and evil deeds . . ."[78] He would not have understood a concept of gentleness and compassion that lacked a backbone of steel. The welfare of the Church and indeed of all mankind was at stake. To me, at least, the evidence I have presented indicates clearly that Bellarmino was greatly concerned that Galileo stop helping error to creep among the flock to the ruin of Catholic truth, and that he stop forthwith. Without denying the irregularities of the disputed document and the difficulties they create, I am nevertheless convinced that on 26 February 1616 Cardinal Bellarmino did in fact do what His Holiness -- at Bellarmino's own insistence, in my understanding -- instructed him to do; that is, he warned Galileo in unmistakable terms to abandon the condemned opinion.

We must not allow ourselves to formulate the events of 1615-16 in misleading terms. It was not ignorance and narrow-mindedness that condemned Copernicanism. Cardinal Bellarmino represented the finest flower of Catholic learning. I myself have come to appreciate his various qualities to a degree quite scandalous in a Presbyterian elder. Far from being ignorant, Bellarmino was the captive, as all of us are captives, of his lifetime's experience, in his case the defense of his Church and of the world view his experience fostered. The tragedy of his Church lay in the fact that he saw the rise of modern science on the analogy of Protestantism and failed to recognize that it was instead a fundamental reshaping of the intellectual landscape within which Christianity, Catholic and Protestant alike, would have henceforth to proceed. In the 13th century, the recovery of Aristotle had presented Christianity with a similar challenge, and Christianity had been able to continue fashioning medieval culture because it learned to state its message in Aristotle's idiom. Beside the earthquake that was the rise of modern science, however, the recovery of Aristotle in the 13th century had been a mere tremor. Bellarmino was of course not by himself the Catholic Church. Institutions cannot make decisions, however, only the individuals who lead them, and I have been arguing, as I am convinced, that Bellarmino was the determinative voice on this issue at that time, though obviously within a context prepared to accept his views. To the misfortune of the Catholic Church Bellarmino failed to recognize what was happening. Locked within his world view, he met the challenge of the rise of modern science with a response that served only, in the end, greatly to injure the institution he wanted above all to defend.

As for Galileo, it is equally mistaken to see in him an enemy of that Church, or in any of the leaders of the new science an enemy of Christianity. It is true that Galileo was not given to spiritual exaltation, but one must not believe that spiritual exaltation is essential to sincere belief. Recall the scene on 23 June 1633, when Galileo stood before the assembled cardinals of the Church and learned to his surprise that he was being forced publicly to abjure Copernicanism. It is probably not true that Galileo had been shown the instruments of torture. He knew what they were without seeing them, and his correspondence makes it clear he was terrified that they might be used on him. He was an old man, almost seventy, who had been seriously ill without much respite for the past twenty years. He knew very well that he did not have the strength to resist those terrible engines and that they could reduce him to jelly in a matter of minutes. He nevertheless told the assembled cardinals that though he would do what they were going to force him to do, he would not say he was not a Catholic because he was one and intended to die one despite his enemies.[79]

Galileo had entered, however, willy-nilly, into the new world shaped by the earthquake then in progress, and everything that Bellarmino saw from his world view looked different from Galileo's. The issue has nothing to do with the relative merits of the two world views. To me they appear incommensurable.   The issue rather is the compulsion exercised by historical reality.   As the Church had remained a central factor in European life for more than fifteen hundred years by refusing ever to put itself in opposition to prevailing learning, so it would remain a factor in the new age then being formed if it refused to be at odds with modern science. The net result of Cardinal Bellarmino's devoted effort to defend his Church was to place an incubus to its back that it struggles still to shake off.

Thus Galileo, who spoke from the perspective of the new world view, had the final word in the exchange. It was 1633 when he uttered it, in a letter to Elia Diodati composed shortly before he travelled to Rome to face his second trial by the Inquisition. Cardinal Bellarmino had been in his grave for more than a decade, and Galileo's words overtly concerned the recent book of Libert Froidmont against Copernicus. I do not find it fanciful to imagine that he had Bellarmino in mind as well.

> When Froidmont or others have established that to say the earth moves is heresy, while demonstrations, observations, and necessary conclusions show that it does move, in what a swamp will he have lost himself and the Holy Church?[80]

Notes

1.   *Le Opere di Galileo Galilei*, ed. naz., ed. Antonio Favaro, 20 vols. (Firenze: Barbéra, 1890-1909), *19*, 323.

2.   Galileo to Mazzoni, 30 May 1597, Galileo to Kepler, 4 Aug. 1597; *ibid., 2*, 197-202 and *10*, 67-8. A letter of Castelli to Galileo, 5 December 1610, (*ibid., 10*, 480-2) was explicitly Copernican and appears to have assumed that it was addressing another acknowledged Copernican. Castelli had been Galileo's student in Padua, and there is every reason to refer the apparently shared conviction to his student years, well before the discoveries with the telescope.

3.   Cigoli to Galileo, 16 December 1611; *ibid., 11*, 241-2.

4.   Galileo's letter to Lorini has been lost, but see Lorini's reply on 5 Nov. 1612; *ibid., 11*, 427.

5.   Castelli to Galileo, 14 Dec. 1613; *ibid., 11*, 606.

6.   Galileo to Castelli, 20 Dec. 1613; *ibid., 5*, 281-8.

7.   See the record of the Inquisition on which I primarily rely for the following narrative; *ibid., 19*, 275-324.

8.   See his deposition in the records of the Inquisition; *ibid., 19*, 307-11.

9.   See the record of the Inquisition; *ibid., 19*, 275-9, 295-324.

10. Galileo to Picchena, 6 Feb. 1616; *ibid., 12*, 230.

11. *Ibid., 19*, 320-1. The wording of the second proposition was not as I have given it, but I take this to have been its meaning.

12. Quoted in James Brodrick, *Robert Bellarmine, Saint and Scholar*, (Westminster: Newman Press, 1961), p. 156.

13. Brodrick quotes at length the contemporary account, by an English priest, Father Edward Coffin, *A True Relation of the last Sickness and Death of Cardinal Bellarmine*, (Saint-Omer, 1622); *ibid.*, pp. 413-21.

14. *Ibid.*, pp. 303-4.

15. Without specific reference to the years 1615-16, Bellarmino listed the two among the Congregations on which he served. *Die Selbstbiographie des Cardinals Bellarmin*, ed. Joh. Jos. Ign. Döllinger and Fr. Heinrich Reusch, (Bonn: Neusser, 1887), p. 44.

16. See Bellarmino to Mercurian (General of the Company of Jesus), 1 Aug. 1573, and Bellarmino to Card. Sirlet, 1 April 1575; Xavier-Marie Le Bachelet, *Bellarmin avant son cardinalat, 1542-1598. Correspondence et documents*, (Paris: Beauchesne, 1911), pp. 84-5 and 90-4. A fragment of the dedication of the *Controveries* to Pope Sixtus V, dated 1586, stated that he had devoted the previous fifteen years to controversies explicating the faith; *ibid.*, pp. 145-6. This chronology extends back nearly to the beginning of the years in Louvain.

17. Chapter II. Seven Years in Louvain; Brodrick, *Bellarmine,* pp. 25-50.

18. See the relevant letters in Le Bachelet, *Bellarmin*, pp. 245-77.

19. Galla Galli, *La Vita e il pensiero di Giordano Bruno*, (Milano: Marzorati, 1973), pp. 44-5.

20. Chapter IX. Trouble with the Republic of Venice; Brodrick, *Bellarmine,* pp. 249-63.

21. *Ibid.*, pp. 279, 294-8.

22. See for example Bellarmino's judgment on the propositions of Jan Jansen, his report on the controversy in Louvain, and his letter to Deckers, 5 Oct. 1591; Le Bachelet, *Bellarmin*, pp. 162-3, 211-13, and 311-13. All of these documents concern the controversy in Louvain, the forerunner of the Jansenist controversy, over free will and efficacious grace. Although Bellarmino supported the Jesuit Leonard Leys (Lessius) in this struggle, he did not hesitate to say, in typical fashion, that Leys's proposition on election seemed "false" to him; *ibid.*, p. 199.

23. Bellarmino to Aquaviva, 27 Dec. 1591 and 28 Jan. 1592; *ibid.*, pp. 317-21 and 326-7.

24. Roberto Bellarmino, *Disputationes Roberti Bellarmini Politiani, S.J., S.R.E. Cardinalis, de controversiis christianae fidei, adversus nostri temporis haereticos*, 4 vols. (Venezia: Malachino, 1721), *1*, Praefatio, n.p. See also the fragment of the dedication of volume one to Pope Sixtus V: With St. Jerome he holds that "there is no one so impious whom a heretic does not exceed in impiety. For because faith is the foundation and source of the whole spiritual structure and of all heavenly benefits, those who labor to take away the faith of the Church, which heretics do, corrupt the entire welfare of the Church at the same time, and strive completely to overthrow the Church itself." (Le Bachelet, *Bellarmin*, p. 145.)

25. Quoted in Brodrick, *Bellarmine*, p. 318.

26. *De controversiis, 1*, Praefatio, n.p.

27. *De verbo dei. Liber primus*, Chap. 1; *ibid..1*, 1.

28. *De verbi dei interpretatione. Liber tertius* (despite the additional word in the title, book three of the first Controversy, *De verbo dei*), especially Chapter 3; *ibid., 1,* 69. Those familiar with Ugo Baldini and George V. Coyne, "The Louvain Lectures (Lectiones Lovanienses) of Bellarmine and the Autograph Copy of his 1616 Declaration to Galileo," *Vatican Observatory Publications: Studi Galileiani, 1.2* (1984), will recognize that I have received and accepted great assistance from the authors in finding relevant sections in Bellarmino's voluminous writings.

29. *De verbo dei non scripto. Liber quartus* (again, despite the two additional words, book four of the first Controversy, *De verbo dei*); I quote here from Chapter 9; *ibid., 1,* 80-94. See also the Fourth Controversy, *De conciliis, et ecclesia militante,* Chapter 14, *2,* 73-4. "The Church is not able to err in any way, not even in forsaking God." He brings up Calvin's restriction of the Church's inerrancy to doctrines explicitly in Scripture and to the church universal as opposed to the present Catholic Church. "However our opinion is that the Church absolutely cannot err, neither in things absolutely necessary nor in other things which it proposes to us to believe or to do, whether they are explicitly set down in the Scriptures or not." The Church (which is of course the present Catholic Church) is governed by Christ as by its head and spouse and by the Holy Spirit as by its soul. They guard it against every error.

30. *Prima (i.e., the first in vol. 2, but really the fourth) controversia generalis. De conciliis, et ecclesia militante,* Chapter 12; *ibid., 2,* 43. To amplify the understanding of the last passage, let me quote the slightly different but not contradictory translation of Baldini and Coyne: "in Scripture not only the meaning but all the words and individual words pertain to faith. For we believe that no word has been inserted in Scripture uselessly or imprecisely." Baldini and Coyne, "Louvain Lectures," p. 40.

31. *Ibid.,* p. 16.

32. *Ibid.,* pp. 18-20.

33. *Ibid.,* p. 22.

34. Quoted in *ibid.,* p. 45.

35. Angelo Mercati, *Il sommario del processo di Giordano Bruno,* (Vatican City: Biblioteca Apostolica Vaticana, 1942), pp. 5-9, 55-119 (especially 79-83). Galli, *Bruno,* p. 45.

36. Mercati, *Sommario,* pp. 7 and 117.

37. Bellarmino's letter to the mathematicians at the *Collegio Romano* on 19 April stated that he had observed the new phenomena through the telescope, though he did not say that Galileo had assisted him; *Opere, 12,* pp. 87-8. In a letter to

Galileo four years later, Piero Dini repeated Bellarmino's recollection of a discussion with Galileo about the discoveries; Dini to Galileo, 15 May 1615; *ibid., 12*, 151.

38.　*Opere, 11*, 87-8, 92-3. English translation in Brodrick, *Bellarmine*, pp. 343-5.

39.　*Ibid., 19*, 275.

40.　Galileo's two letters to Conti do not survive; I infer their content from Conti's replies. Conti to Galileo, 7 July and 18 Aug. 1612; *ibid., 11*, 354-5 and 376.

41.　*Ibid., 5*, 138-9. Galileo had become familiar with the Scriptural passages in question some twenty years earlier in the course of digesting the lecture notes of professors of natural philosophy at the *Collegio Romano*. William A. Wallace, *Galileo's Early Notebooks: the Physical Questions*, (Notre Dame: Univ. of Notre Dame Press, 1977), pp. 94, 101-2.

42.　Cesi to Galileo between 24 Nov. 1612 and 26 Jan. 1613; *ibid., 11*, 437-72 passim.

43.　This is what Galileo stated in his letter to Msgr. Piero Dini, 16 Feb. 1615; *Opere, 5*, 292.

44.　In a letter to Galileo on 4 October 1614, Cesi said that he was about to leave for Acquasparta. His correspondence shows that he was there from that time until the beginning of the following March, restricted in his movements by his concern over the illness of his wife, who would die without recovering on 1 November 1615. Giuseppe Gabrieli, "Il carteggio linceo della vecchia accademia di Federico Cesi," *Memorie della R. Accademia Nazionale dei Lincei, Classe di scienze morali, storiche e filologiche, ser. VI, 7.1*, (1938), 462-87.

45.　Cesi to Galileo, 12 Jan. 1615; *ibid., 12*, 128-31.

46.　Galileo to Dini, 16 Feb. 1615; *ibid., 5*, 292.

47.　Galileo to Castelli, 21 Dec. 1613; *Opere, 5*, 282. The letter to Castelli became the first draft of the well known *Letter to Madame Christina of Lorraine, Grand Duchess of Tuscany*, which Stillman Drake has translated, *Discoveries and Opinions of Galileo*, (Garden City, N.Y.: Doubleday, 1957), pp. 175-216. Galileo copied much of the letter to Castelli verbatim into the *Letter to the Grand Duchess Christina*, and I will use Drake's translations, modified where differences in the original Italian texts make it necessary, as in this case. The modestly different form of this passage appears in *Discoveries and Opinions*, p. 181.

48.　*Opere, 5*, 282. *Discoveries and Opinions*, p. 182.

49.　*Opere, 5*, 282. *Discoveries and Opinions*, p. 181.

50.　*Opere, 5*, 282. *Discoveries and Opinions*, p. 182.

51.　*Opere, 5*, 283. *Discoveries and Opinions*, p. 186.

52. *Opere, 5*, 284. Castelli corrected Galileo's imperfect knowledge of Scripture on this point; the *Letter to the Grand Duchess* said that the Bible mentioned only Venus; *Discoveries and Opinions*, p. 184.

53. *Opere, 5*, 284. *Discoveries and Opinions*, p. 183.

54. *Opere, 5*, 284. *Discoveries and Opinions*, p. 187.

55. *Opere, 5*, 285. *Discoveries and Opinions*, p. 209.

56. *Opere, 5*, 286-7. *Discoveries and Opinions*, pp. 211-15.

57. A translation of the letter into English appears in Thomas Salusbury, *Mathematical Collections and Translations*, a reissue of vol. 1 of the original publication, (London: Leybourn, 1667), Pt. 1, pp. 473-503.

58. Bellarmino to Foscarini, 12 April 1615; *Opere, 12*, 171-2. It is translated in full in Brodrick, *Bellarmine*, pp 362-3, from which I quote. Msgr. Dini sent a copy to Galileo on 18 April; *Opere, 12*, 173.

59. Pierre Duhem, *To Save the Phenomena: an Essay on the Idea of Physical Theory from Plato to Galileo*, tr. Edmund Doland and Chaninah Maschler, (Chicago: Univ. of Chicago Press, 1969), pp. 104-12. The original was published in France in 1908. See also Duhem, *The Aim and Structure of Physical Theory*, tr. Philip P. Wiener, (Princeton: Princeton Univ. Press, 1954), p. 43. The original French edition of this work appeared in 1906.

60. *Opere, 19*, 320-1.

61. *Discoveries and Opinions*, p. 191.

62. Galileo to Picchena, 23 Jan. 1616; *Opere, 12*, 227-8.

63. *Discoveries and Opinions*. pp. 191-7.

64. *Ibid.*, p. 206.

65. *Ibid.*, p. 209. See also analogous texts on pp. 175, 176, 196, 197, 199, 200.

66. *Ibid.*, pp. 202-3.

67. *Ibid.*, p. 215.

68. Brodrick, *Bellarmine*, p. 382.

69. *The Mind's Ascent to God by a Ladder of Created Things*, tr. Monialis, (London: Mowbray, 1925), p. 4.

70. *Ibid.*, p. 106.

71. *Ibid.*, p. 124.

72.   *Opere, 19,* 278.

73.   The Tuscan ambassador to Rome, Niccolini, repeated the claim in a letter to the court in Florence, 13 Nov. 1632; *ibid., 14,* 428.

74.   References to the "League of Pigeons," Galileo's derisory title for the group lead by Ludoviso delle Colombe, appear in his correspondence in connection with the controversy over his *Discourse on Bodies in Water.* See Galileo to Cesi, 5 Jan. 1613, and Cigoli to Galileo, 1 Feb. 1613; *ibid., 11,* 461 and 476.

75.   I refer to its use of the verb "serpere." The verb is not a very common one. I can recall only one other place where I have seen it, the preface to Bellarmino's *Controversies,* in which he speaks of how the venom of heresy, infecting a hundred others for every one it kills, "creeps [serpit]" far and wide. (*De controversiis,* Praefatio, n.p.) The context was identical in the two places, and the verb, with its evocation of the scene in the Garden of Eden, was peculiarly appropriate to Bellarmino's purpose in both.

76.   *Opere, 19,* 321-2.

77.   I take such an assumption to be implicit, for example, in the treatments of Giorgio di Santillana, *The Crime of Galileo,* (Chicago: Univ. of Chicago Press, 1955), pp. 242-3, and Stillman Drake, *Galileo at Work,* (Chicago: Univ. of Chicago Press, 1978), pp. 252-5.

78.   *The Mind's Ascent,* pp. 76-7.

79.   The account of the trial by Giovanfrancesco Buonamici, July 1633; *Opere, 19,* 411. See Giorgio Spini, "The Rationale of Galileo's Religiousness," in *Galileo Reappraised,* ed. Carlo L. Golino, (Berkeley and Los Angeles: Univ. of California Press, 1966), pp. 44-66; and the same article in its original Italian, "La religiosità di Galileo," in *Saggi su Galileo Galilei,* ed. Carlo Maccagni, (Firenze: Barbéra, 1972), *2,* 416-40.

80.   Galileo to Diodati, 15 Jan. 1633; *Opere, 15,* 25.

GALILEO AND THE JESUITS

On 7 August 1632, Filippo Magalotti wrote to his friend Mario Guiducci in Florence. Magalotti had recently arrived in Rome with eight copies of Galileo's *Dialogue*, among the first copies of the book to reach the Papal city because of an interruption of communications caused by the plague. He reported that Niccolo Riccardi, the Master of the Sacred Palace, the ultimate censor of the church and thus the man who had licensed the *Dialogue* for publication, had hunted him out and asked him to hand them over. It was too late. They were presentation copies, and as Riccardi well knew, since he was the recipient of one, Magalotti had already distributed them. Why did he make such a request? Riccardi had evaded the query with a ridiculous objection to the frontispiece, but Magalotti indicated to Guiducci that the overt objection was the *Dialogue's* conclusion, which did not assert the supremacy of faith over scientific reason vigorously enough. "This is the pretext," Magalotti continued, "but the reality must be that the Jesuit Fathers are working behind the scene with all their strength to have the book banned, for he [Riccardi] himself said as much to me in these words: The Jesuits will pursue him with extreme bitterness."[1]

Magalotti's letter was among the earliest indications Galileo received that trouble was brewing, trouble that would lead him during the following year into the Inquisition's prison, impose on him a public abjuration of Copernicanism, and condemn him to house arrest for the remaining decade of his life. The trial of Galileo was one of the epochal events of the seventeenth century, an enduring symbol of the tension between two different systems of thought as modern science began to displace Christianity from the focus of Western civilization. And in Magalotti's letter, which is among the earliest words pointing directly toward it that we have, the Jesuits stand at the center of attention. Galileo never ceased to believe that the Jesuits had been the leading authors of his troubles.[2] He was not alone. It was the accepted wisdom of the day, a judgment endlessly repeated.[3]

Manifestly, Galileo's relations with the Jesuits are a historical question of some importance. It should be clear, first of all, that a divergence of belief about ultimate intellectual authority and the role of Christian revelation in science did separate them. Consider the implications of a letter that Galileo received from Guiducci late in May, 1633. Late May was the very climax of the trial. As Galileo was being tormented (not physically, to be sure) by the Inquisition in Rome, his native Florence, and the whole of northern Italy, were being tormented by the plague, the same visitation of the plague familiar to many from the pages of Manzoni's *I promessi sposi*. "In regard to health," Guiducci reported, "the situation is slowly improving, and there have not been as many deaths as we have written about [earlier]. This morning the Holy Madonna of Impruneta was brought to Florence, and she will stay here until Monday. The hope vested in this image, which has always been so miraculous in succoring this city, is very great, and the people have conceived the greatest hope that through the intercession of the Holy Virgin we will remain free [of the plague]. May it please the Lord God that we have prepared ourselves in such a way as not to be unworthy of so much assistance."[4]

Who can doubt that we stand before an historic threshold whereby Western civilization passed (not with a single step, of course) from one world view, represented here by the Inquisition and the Madonna, into another, represented by Galileo and modern science? Who can doubt, for that matter, that the Jesuits perceived more clearly than Galileo what the ultimate impact of modern science upon Christianity would be? And if it is understanding we pursue, we must not permit ourselves to wonder that the Jesuits were ready to defend that world in which they lived and moved and had their being.

I am convinced that an issue of belief, associated with that transformation of world view, lay at the very core of the trial of Galileo. Great historical events have many dimensions, however. Galileo and the Jesuits pursued their evolving relations within the context of a specific society in which the system of patronage supported all of the higher culture as it supported Galileo himself. Without in any way denying the importance of the issue of belief, I seek here to explore how far the perspective provided by the system of patronage can help to illuminate Galileo's relations with the Jesuits. My phrase is "help to illuminate." Galileo and the Jesuits lived in a complex society in which many factors beyond the question of belief to which I have referred and the system of patronage contributed to shape men's actions. The best one can do is to isolate for examination individual features without forgetting that they were single strands in an intricate web. My intention is to enquire how far the system of patronage can help to illuminate a matter as complex as epochal events are wont to be.

Galileo and the System of Patronage

Galileo burst on the intellectual scene in 1609 when he was already forty-five years old. To those who had known him, his sudden emergence was no surprise, for he had been a witty conversationalist and an exhilarating teacher, one of those rare men capable of galvanizing his companions with his brilliance. Nevertheless, beyond two narrow circles in Venice and Padua and in Florence, his very existence had scarcely been known. Except for a small pamphlet describing the operation of a calculating device he had improved, and a later defense of his priority with the device, he had not published anything, and in that age as surely as now, those who did not publish perished. Then, in 1609-10, came the telescope and the observations of the heavens announced in the *Sidereus Nuncius*.

It is not possible, I am convinced, to overestimate the impact of the telescopic discoveries. Galileo was revealing the existence of a wholly new world, a new world not only unknown but not dreamed of before, even by the ancients. Correspondents vied with each other in plundering history and mythology for the image that could appropriately describe its discoverer -- Columbus, Magellan, Atlas. Ontioco Bentivogli, who admitted that he had not originally believed the claims, found himself forced to confess that Galileo, "not only like Linceus, but like another Prometheus, has truly mounted to the heavens and penetrated their most profound secrets; so that I thank God that by your means He has been pleased to let me also participate in the knowledge of things so rare and concealed for so many ages."[5] After his visit to Rome in 1611, Galileo received a letter from his friend Paolo Gualdo, citing a letter Gualdo had received from Mark Welser in Augsburg. Welser had described in detail a banquet given to honor Galileo in Rome. As Gualdo commented, Galileo was now watched and reported throughout the world.[6]

The telescope and the *Sidereus Nuncius* were not, of course, the end of Galileo's achievement. He quickly consolidated their promise with two more books, and later there would be much more. To us, looking back from more than three and a half centuries, the discoveries with the telescope seem almost the least of Galileo's accomplishments. This was not the case in his own age. The great works we think of immediately when his name is mentioned, the *Dialogue* and the *Discourses*, were the products of the final years of a long life, and their impact was felt primarily by later periods. In his own time, Galileo's badge of genius was the telescope. Instantly it transformed him into the most celebrated intellectual of Italy, and probably of Europe. And it transformed him as well into one of the most desirable clients, a man likely to bring glory to the patron who supported his activity.

It is essential to my theme that Galileo comprehended the system of patronage and knew how to exploit it. He demonstrated his knowledge of the system from the very beginning, with the *Sidereus Nuncius*. That treatise was literally born on the night, 11 January 1610, when Galileo realized that the stars he had discovered near Jupiter were satellites circling the planet. As we know from his correspondence, he had been seeking to leave Padua, to escape from the burdens of teaching, to find leisure to pursue his research and to write; and as we also know, he had concluded that only the patronage of an absolute prince could supply him with these benefits. Galileo named the satellites for the ruling family of his native Florence and composed the *Sidereus Nuncius,* which he dedicated to the Grand Duke, to proclaim their existence to the world. For his pains, he was appointed Professor of Mathematics at the University of Pisa, without obligation to teach or to reside in Pisa, and Mathematician and Philosopher to the Grand Duke, with an annual stipend of one thousand scudi. To the court in Florence, Galileo expressed the fear that the rest of the world might doubt the existence of the Medicean stars if they had to accept them on his authority alone. In order for the Grand Duke to gain the maximum esteem from the new celestial bodies that bore his name, it was essential for others to see the satellites for themselves. Hence he had prepared a number of excellent telescopes for the other rulers of Europe, so that they might know by their own eyes that the Medicean planets were real, though he would send the telescopes only at the Grand Duke's orders, an inspired maneuver whereby Galileo enlisted the Grand Duke as his public relations agent.[7]

With his following publications, Galileo took care to send copies to the wealthy and powerful, especially to Cardinals of the Church. In the twentieth century, scholars advertise their achievements by sending presentation copies to academic colleagues. In the early seventeenth century, under the system of patronage, Galileo sent presentation copies to potential patrons. As far as possible, he timed his visits to Rome to maximize their effect. Thus he paid his first visit (after the advent of the telescope) only when he had a new discovery of great importance, the phases of Venus. The following visit, of which we shall hear, was not entirely spontaneous; but on the next one, in 1624, he carried microscopes with him, one of which we know he presented to Cardinal von Zollern for the Duke of Bavaria. "I saw a fly that Signor Galileo himself arranged for me to see," Johannes Faber, a prominent member of the *Accademia dei Lincei* reported to Federico Cesi, the *Principe* of the *Accademia*. "I was astonished, and said to Signor Galileo that he was another Creator since he made things appear that until now were not known to have been created."[8] On responses such as that a career could rest secure.

During the critical years of Galileo's career, however, microscopes and books that he published were secondary. The telescope remained the foundation of his enormous reputation. Until the late 1630's, not many years before his death, Galileo's telescopes remained the best that were made, and he continued to receive requests for them until the end of his life. Some of the instruments went to fellow investigators; for example, Gassendi sought and obtained one, though he was careful to indicate that Peiresc was involved in the request.[9] The overwhelming majority of them, however, went to men of the patron class, like Peiresc, rather than other scientists. Thus, toward the end of 1629, Galileo received a request for a telescope for Phillip IV, the King of Spain, with the information that the court insisted on paying, without further ado, whatever price Galileo set. At that time Galileo was completing the *Dialogue*. Nevertheless, he immediately undertook the preparation of an instrument suitable for the King of Spain. As to payment, he humbly begged to inform His Majesty that he could not similarly serve him. He had never, Galileo stated, accepted payment for a telescope, and he never intended to.[10] From the evidence I have seen, the assertion appears to have been true. Do not be misled to conclude that the action was disinterested. The adventurer from Flanders who came to Venice with the instrument that launched Galileo's career had tried to sell it to the Senate. Galileo had presented his improved version to the Doge and thereby made his fortune. He never forgot the lesson.

In such particulars we begin to perceive the material circumstances within which Galileo was able to pursue a life of science that could not easily have supported him otherwise in the early seventeenth century. He could, it is true, have stayed on in Padua, though a university chair, which demanded periodic reappointment, with decisions made by men of precisely the same dominant class, differed less from the world of patronage than one might at first think. Galileo's decision to leave Padua, the decision of a man without personal means, was a decision to throw himself wholly into the world of patronage. Activities such as the presentation of books and of telescopes to men of wealth and power were the social reality of the day, and by accepting their necessity and conforming to the limits they set, Galileo was able to realize his magnificent achievement.

We can contemplate in this respect a letter that Galileo received from Benedetto Castelli in 1638. Castelli had been in Rome for more than a decade in the service of the Barberini, the Papal family, and through their influence he had been appointed to the chair in mathematics at the university in Rome. In 1638, when a death vacated the chair in mathematics at the University of Pisa, where Castelli had once taught with distinction, the Grand Duke attempted to lure him back. Castelli was anxious that he not offend the Grand Duke, but he also could not accept his proposal. In his letter of 30 July, he explained to Galileo why he could not. He was, Castelli reminded Galileo, a member of the Cassino Congregation of the Benedictine Order, subject to the "protection" of Cardinal Francesco Barberini, the powerful nephew of the Pope, and he was as well in the personal service of the Cardinal. "I have no way to free myself from this place," Castelli continued, "without the danger of ruining my affairs in a way that I could never reverse." Six months earlier, Castelli's enemies had sent a monk to Rome to seek his professorship, a man who had some qualifications and warm recommendations to Cardinal Barberini. Only on the day of the letter had Castelli received his reappointment; he had to walk with caution and not give any offense.[11]

Castelli's letter is a perfect expression of the dependence of a client on the good will and pleasure of his patron, even in the case of Galileo, whose achievements supplied him with some leverage. The relation between patron and client was not solely economic. It involved recognition, prestige, and standing in society. But along with these benefits the relation was also economic; and men such as Castelli and Galileo, who did not possess personal wealth, were not at liberty to ignore the economic realities. Galileo was attractive to the Grand Duke in direct proportion as he was attractive to the class of patrons as a whole. The Grand Duke displayed his magnificence by supporting a client with whom every patron would have been delighted to see his name associated. Requests for telescopes from Cardinals and from the King of Spain were of maximum utility to Galileo. They were absolutely necessary. Without them he was nothing. Galileo understood as much and acted accordingly.

Conflict and Denunciation

Meanwhile, he was not the only hopeful man making his way in early seventeenth century society, and other potential clients were not necessarily as exhilarated at Galileo's success as he was. Galileo himself was always convinced that their envy and malice, as he repeatedly expressed it, was the source of all his troubles. There appears to have been a large measure of truth in his assessment.

Soon after he arrived in Florence, Galileo became engaged in a dispute at some social gathering. Apparently he was the aggressor. Anxious as he was to display his brilliance, he was only too ready to pounce on a statement by an Aristotelian philosopher that ice is condensed water, and the discussion quickly expanded into a debate on why bodies float. Galileo's opponents were convinced that he was wrong and that they could use the incident to destroy his credibility with the Grand Duke. The leading spokesman of the group was a lecturer at the University of Pisa named Ludovico delle Colombe. "Colombe" is the Italian for "dove"; hence one finds references in Galileo's correspondence at this time to the League of Pigeons, that is, Galileo's opponents.[12]

Out of the dispute came Galileo's second major publication, the *Discourse on Bodies in Water*, a treatise which brought the mathematical principles of Archimedean hydrostatics to bear on the categories of Aristotelian natural philosophy. I wish to follow this controversy only in so far as it concerns the question of patronage. Four replies to Galileo's *Discourse* appeared. All of them were composed by academics at the University of Pisa. All of them were dedicated to one or another member of the Medici family. According to one assertion by Galileo, their authors bound themselves together (hence the notion of a league), before his own *Discourse* appeared, to oppose whatever he might say in it.[13] That is, by every indication, we have to do with a struggle within the system of patronage. As Arturo d'Elci, the Overseer of the university, who wrote one of the attacks under the pseudonym of "The Unknown Academician," expressed it, Galileo was "greedy for glory," and d'Elci clearly feared that Galileo's assertiveness was bound to infringe on the welfare of established clients like himself.[14]

A further indication that the controversy arose out of the issue of patronage appears in a letter from Castelli. The time of these events preceded the letter from Castelli that I quoted above by twenty-five years; Castelli had just been appointed to a professorship of mathematics at the University of Pisa. In one of his earliest letters to Galileo from Pisa, he sent the greetings of an anatomist, Ruschio, who suggested very strongly (as Castelli put it, "in block letters") that Galileo was not envied "for the great and marvelous achievements of his intellect, matters that do not fall within the knowledge or the consideration of these malicious men, but for those thousand scudi [Galileo's stipend from the Grand Duke], which are probably better known by them and more avidly desired than by you."[15]

Let me pause briefly with the controversy over bodies in water because it revealed two features of Galileo that are relevant both to patronage as a whole and to his later relations with the Jesuits. The first of these features is Galileo's ego. To describe it as king-sized is seriously to understate it. There is a passage, for example, from the *Reply* to his critics, which was published in 1615 without an author's name but with Castelli's signature attached to the dedication. From the surviving manuscript, we know that Galileo composed most of it, though Castelli composed its opening section, which Galileo then revised thoroughly. From the manuscript we can identify the author of each individual phrase. Thus, at one point, Castelli wrote that Colombe, in trying to destroy Galileo, has in fact bestowed the highest praise on him, for Colombe celebrates the discoverers of new things and compares them to the Gods, and Castelli added that among the discoverers of new things Galileo was, by common agreement, appropriately included. Galileo amended the passage by the insertion of one adverb, "meritamente," so that it now read: "and *properly* compares them to the Gods . . ."[16]

Add to his ego, perhaps as one facet of it, his inability to carry on a controversy in a civil manner. Colombe's pamphlet against Galileo was hardly a model of civility, and one can scarcely wonder that he chose to reply in kind. The other three objections to Galileo's treatise, however, remained properly on a plane of philosophic discourse and refrained from any appeal to personal invective. One cannot, alas, say the same about Galileo's reply. It was addressed throughout *ad hominem*. Its basic instrument was ridicule. It is impossible, in my opinion, to read it without concluding that Galileo's aim was less to establish the truth of the issue under discussion than absolutely to humiliate his opponents. "There is no point," he exclaimed, "in undertaking to refute someone who is so ignorant that it would require a huge volume to refute his stupidities (which number more than the lines of his essay) . . ."[17] Perhaps there was no point in the exercise, but he performed it nevertheless. To pamphlets of 50 pages he replied with a volume of 350. A grenade had been exploded outside his door; for his response, nothing less than a bomb could assuage his outrage.

These are not easy matters for a historian of science to discuss. There is no doubt in my mind that Galileo had good cause for his ego. He was one of the handful of rare geniuses that have graced mankind. His four opponents in the controversy were not even close to the same calibre. My goal at this point, however, is not to assess relative merits but to comprehend Galileo's impact on his contemporaries. We have a word for his conduct, and we should not fear to use it. Galileo was insufferable.

And what is important to my argument, the characteristics that made him insufferable were not solely personal. They were also intimately related to patronage. Where certain institutional arrangements lead one to disguise and suppress his egotism and contempt for others, patronage encouraged these characteristics in Galileo. It does not seem much too strong to say that patronage demanded them.

It is relevant, surely, that humanistic controversies of that period, involving men who worked within the same system, frequently displayed similar features. And it is revealing that Galileo's young followers, identifying with his status as the Grand Duke's philosopher, quickly learned to ape his manners. Thus Niccolo Aggiunti lamented the "calumnies and impostures of malicious men" that afflicted Galileo; and without reflecting apparently on what generated malice toward Galileo, went on to describe Chiaramonti's book on the stability of the earth, which in fact he had not even seen yet, as "this excrement of a melancholy humor."[18] Galileo was attractive as a client exactly in so far as he was perceived as a godlike discoverer of new things and a brilliant philosopher who easily outshone his opponents in philosophic discourse. The praise heaped upon him by men of the highest rank, their gifts, his special appointment by the Grand Duke, did nothing to diminish his self-esteem. Egotism may have come easily to Galileo, but he received every possible stimulus to behave as he did.

While the controversy on bodies in water was still in progress, Galileo became involved in a second one, which did not address itself to the Tuscan scene but nevertheless involved matters that bear on my topic. The opponent in the new controversy, which concerned sunspots, was a German who wrote under the pseudonym of Apelles. Their differences involved the interpretation of the spots seen on or in front of the sun, with manifold opportunities for sarcastic thrusts like those mentioned above; and they included as well the question of priority in the discovery, with all of the potential for bitterness that such questions seem usually to entail. Galileo eventually learned that Apelles was Christopher Scheiner, a Jesuit whom the order called to Rome in 1624. Although Scheiner does not seem initially to have looked upon Galileo as an enemy, he was not one quietly to swallow ridicule, and when he did learn to hate Galileo, he remained implacable until his death.

Soon there was a third controversy as well. Like the first, this one began in Tuscany, though it soon spread beyond. In December of 1613, the court was in Pisa, and Castelli, then in the early months of his appointment to the university, was present at a state dinner. It is surely significant that the incident took place at the court, a firm indication that the controversy began as another attempt to undermine Galileo with his patron. The Grand Duchess Christina of Lorraine, the widow of Ferdinand I and the mother of Cosimo, was a very pious woman, too pious by twice for Galileo's good. During the dinner a cleric was whispering in her ear. When Castelli was about to leave, he was called back and forced into a discussion of the Copernican system and Scripture, a discussion in which it was clear to all that Castelli stood as the representative of Galileo. There had been suggestions before that Galileo's enemies might employ the theological weapon against him. With the dinner at the court in Pisa in December 1613, the issue was directly joined.

Castelli wrote to Galileo about the incident at once and received in reply a long letter discussing the question Castelli had been forced to debate, a letter that functioned as the first draft of the well known "Letter to the Grand Duchess Christina."[19] The Bible is the word of God, Galileo argued, and as such it cannot err. Interpreters of the Bible are human, however, and prone to error like all human beings. Nature is also the revelation of God, and nature is its own interpreter. It is immutable and never errs. Fallible men must not endanger the Church by committing it on matters of natural philosophy, which it is not the purpose of the Scriptures to teach, where scientific reason may one day demonstrate the truth of conclusions that they have declared to be false from the evidence of Scripture. What really made Galileo insufferable was the clarity of his understanding, in this case greater clarity than the combined assembly of theologians pursuing their own discipline.

For a year, nothing more happened, at least nothing overt, though apparently copies of the letter to Castelli circulated. Galileo, who never thought poorly of his own compositions and had the original letter after Castelli returned it, must have been responsible for the copies. Then, in December 1614, a Dominican friar, Tommaso Caccini, was preaching in Florence on the book of *Joshua*. When he came to the famous passage, "Sun, stand thou still," he launched into a denunciation of Galileo, Copernicans, and mathematicians in general. Caccini proceeded to denounce the letter to the Inquisition in Florence. When nothing happened, another opponent, Niccolo Lorini, sent the letter to the Inquisition in Rome in February 1615.

This was no joking matter. Galileo was literally beside himself with anxiety, as he had good reason to be. From the record of the Inquisition we know that they pursued the charge, taking depositions.[20] For his part, Galileo mobilized his influential friends in Rome. The details at this stage need not detain us. Suffice it to say that late in 1615, as the case neared its climax, Galileo travelled to Rome to defend himself. He remained in the Papal city for nearly six months. It appears to me that those six months must have been crucial in his relations with the Jesuits.

The Society of Jesus

The period in question, from December 1615 through May 1616, came after six years of the most spectacular success on Galileo's part. At this point the trajectory of his career, mounting almost vertically, intersected another trajectory, that of the Society of Jesus. It is essential to understand that their success had been equally spectacular. The Society of Jesus had been founded three quarters of a century earlier, in 1540, seventy-five years of almost uninterrupted triumphs. As one historian of the order has asserted, the Jesuits had literally changed the course of history.[21] When the order was founded, the Catholic Church was falling back in disarray before the Protestant onslaught. By 1615, the momentum had reversed its direction, and the only question left to be decided was whether Protestantism would survive the counterattack. More than any other factor, the Jesuits had determined that change of direction in the course of events. Within the Catholic world their prestige was enormous.

Moreover, the Jesuit enterprise was uniquely educational and intellectual. Such had not been Loyola's original conception of the order he established. He had thought of the Jesuits as the shock troops of the Pope in the battle against infidelity, wherever its challenge might be. In the middle of the sixteenth century, there was not much doubt about the principal challenge. It was the Protestant movement in Europe. In relation to Protestantism, Loyola and other early Jesuits perceived almost at once the necessity of an educational effort, for it was exactly on the academic front that the Catholic religion was losing the battle. The original Jesuit schools appeared during the first decade of the order's history, and the undertaking underwent an incredible expansion. In the early seventeenth century, more than three quarters of the Jesuit houses were schools and more than four-fifths of the Jesuits themselves were teachers. By 1615, the Jesuits operated more than three hundred colleges, not colleges in the twentieth century American use of the word, but rather gymnasia, though more than a handful of them had university level divisions.[22] By the seventeenth century, the Jesuits had established an educational and intellectual hegemony within the Catholic world.

Special significance attached to one institution in the Jesuit educational enterprise, the *Collegio Romano*. Loyola himself had founded the *Collegio Romano* in 1551 to be at once the crucible in which Jesuit educational practices would be tried and the show piece of the order's educational effort.   To the *Collegio Romano* the order called its best minds.   Here Francisco Suarez, the greatest of the neoscholastic theologians, taught for a number of years.   Here Roberto Bellarmino, the greatest Catholic apologist, pursued most of his career.   Suarez and Bellarmino were by no means the only men of repute.   In the early years of the seventeenth century, the *Collegio Romano* was the most prestigious university in the Catholic world, or better perhaps, in the Christian world.[23]

It is necessary to add, moreover, that Jesuit success in the educational and intellectual world had not been tied to a dogged reassertion of tradition but rather to a ready embrace of what in the new appeared to be good. This was so especially in regard to the humanities. Loyola, and the Jesuit order following him, rejected the concept of a tension between the new learning and Christianity, and thought rather in terms of a full accommodation between the two, indeed of a fusion of them into a true Christian humanism. By the end of the sixteenth century, the Jesuits had become the primary teachers of the humanities in Catholic Europe. Nor had they excluded the exact sciences from their domain. Jesuits schools placed more emphasis on mathematics and applied mathematical sciences, such as astronomy, than any educational system before them had done. When Gregory XIII had set out to reform the calendar, he had turned to an astronomer at the *Collegio Romano*, Christopher Clavius, who became the architect of the Gregorian calendar.[24]E

It does appear to me that the Jesuit concept of a fusion of the traditional and the new bore the seeds of a potential conflict with Galileo, who was convinced that the old order, as far as natural philosophy was concerned, had simply collapsed and needed to be replaced. The Jesuits sought to employ the new learning to bolster the old. In natural philosophy, they were wedded to Aristotle, whose philosophy they saw as the foundation of Scholastic theology, the intellectual rampart of the Catholic religion. Galileo, in contrast, was the vitriolic critic of Aristotelian natural philosophy throughout most of his career. Their difference in outlook was a ready source of probable friction.

In this essay, however, I am concentrating on a different level of interaction. With the Jesuits the issue was not, as it was in Florence, a competition for largess. The Jesuits' ability to command resources within the Catholic world was beyond challenge, and I have not seen any evidence to suggest that Galileo's competition worried them in this respect. As I indicated above, patronage involved prestige and standing as well as money. What seems crucial to me is the fact that Galileo saw himself as the prophet of the new intellectual order in natural philosophy. The Jesuits, on the other hand, against the background of their own history of success, were not inclined to sit quietly at lessons under any human master.

The Jesuits and Galileo

The period of six months in 1615-16 was not Galileo's first contact with the Jesuits. Far from it. By that time his relations with them already stretched back over a quarter of a century. The earliest surviving correspondence of Galileo is an exchange of letters with Christopher Clavius, and subsequent letters indicate that the two had stayed in contact.[25] Moreover, recent scholarship has established the deep influence of the *Collegio Romano* on Galileo. The scholarship to which I refer appears to me to constitute the most significant step toward a fuller understanding of Galileo taken during the last decade. We have long known about some early manuscripts, which were partially published in the *edizione nazionale* under the title, "Juvenilia."[26] As a result of recent studies, we now recognize that these manuscripts depended directly on the lecture notes of professors of philosophy at the *Collegio Romano,* and because we can date the manuscripts from what we know about the faculty at the *Collegio,* we know that they were not juvenile exercises. Rather they were the work of a mature young scholar who was either already a professor at the University of Pisa or at least on the verge of assuming that position, and who turned to the philosophers of the *Collegio Romano* to enhance his understanding of logic and natural philosophy.[27]

No doubt there will be a long discussion about the interpretation of these findings; the findings themselves appear to be established beyond the possibility of rejection. On the basis of what has been published so far, I am impressed by the case that has been made for the enduring influence of the *Collegio Romano* on Galileo's outlook in the allied fields of epistemology and method; I am less impressed with the present case for their enduring influence on his natural philosophy. For this paper, all that matters is the solidly substantiated conclusion that at the beginning of his professional career, Galileo sought out the Jesuit professors of the *Collegio* and willingly placed himself at their feet.

In 1610, Galileo published his short tract, *Sidereus Nuncius,* which asserted the existence of hitherto unknown bodies in the heavens, on the basis of observations made with an instrument that no one else had. Not surprisingly, there was skepticism about his assertion, and not surprisingly there were some who claimed that the new celestial bodies were delusions generated by the instrument itself. It was the Jesuit astronomers at the *Collegio Romano* who obtained a telescope, confirmed Galileo's observations, and said as much publicly. Their support was a critical factor in his initial success.

When Galileo came to Rome in 1611, the *Collegio* organized a special assembly in his honor with a discourse on his discoveries. In addition to the learned community of Rome, a number of counts, dukes and prelates, including at least three Cardinals, attended the assembly, which was little short of an official laying on of hands. Late in 1614, the French cleric, Jean Tarde, visited the *Collegio Romano*. He recorded in his diary that the Jesuit fathers accepted everything Galileo had discovered, including apparently the sunspots, although they agreed that this evidence of mutability in the heavens was the source of some pain.[28] Tarde's visit to Rome fell on the very eve of Galileo's denunciation to the Inquisition. The denunciation was not the work of the Jesuits, who appear on the whole to have been embarrassed by the outburst of Dominican fundamentalism. At least one expression of private support from their number has survived, and among Galileo's letters there are numerous indications that he considered them to be his allies. When fear that the copy of his letter to Castelli sent to Rome by Lorini had been altered to his disadvantage led him to send a copy he knew to be authentic, Galileo specified more than once that he wanted Father Grienberger, the successor to Clavius, to see it.[29] The Jesuit order was not so authoritarian that it contained no diversity of opinion. Nevertheless, I find the evidence very strong that at this stage the members of the Society in Rome who were most influential in such matters were willing to accept Galileo's discoveries. Without denying the basic difference in outlook mentioned above, I am convinced that we should not seek the origin of the conflict between Galileo and the Jesuits solely in Galileo's discoveries themselves, despite the unsettling implications he drew from them.

Against this background consider a lecture delivered at the *Collegio Romano* two years later, on the three comets that had appeared in the heavens in 1618. The man who delivered the lecture was Orazio Grassi, the professor of mathematics at the *Collegio*. Grassi was the Signor Sarsi of *Il Saggiatore*, where Galileo reduced him to an object of derision forever. But Grassi was not an object of derision. He was one of the most respected scientists of the Jesuit order, who occupied the chair in mathematics at the *Collegio Romano* for more than ten years. When the canonization of Loyola led the *Collegio* to plan a new church, St. Ignatius, intended to be second in magnificence in Rome only to St. Peter's, it designated Grassi as the architect. Contrary to the implication of Galileo's ridicule, Grassi was clearly a man of ability much respected by his age.

His lecture on comets did not explicitly mention Galileo. He obviously referred to Galileo several times, however, and the references were all respectful. Nevertheless, Galileo regarded the lecture as an attack, and it appears to me that Galileo was correct. The result of the Church's actions in 1616 (to which I shall return) had been to separate the realms of science and faith. As Bellarmine stated several times, it was permissible to accept the Copernican system as a superior mathematical hypothesis. What was not permissible was the assertion that Coperni-canism is true, for passages in Scripture appeared to be in contradiction to the heliocentric system. Increasingly, moreover, in the opinion of the learned community Galileo had established himself as the recognised master of the separate realm of science. What was the import of Grassi's lecture? Grassi did not build his argument on Scriptural citations. Rather he confined himself to the domain of science and attempted to use the evidence of the comets to demonstrate scientifically that the earth is at the center of the universe, that is, that the very position with which Galileo, in his numerous assertions about the system of the world since 1610, had virtually identified his reputation in science was wrong.[30] Grassi even used the evidence of telescopic observations, invading Galileo's unique territory and turning his own instrument against him.

Thus when Giovanni Rinuccini reported the lecture to Galileo, he added that the Jesuits (and he did use their name in the plural) were claiming that the lecture destroyed the basis of Copernicanism.[31] As Galileo would state his reaction to Grassi's endeavor later, he was "desirous of stripping me and entirely despoiling me of every ornament of glory . . . transported by the desire to obscure my name in the field of science . . ."[32] In his report to Galileo, Rinuccini also added that Galileo would comprehend how much he awaited his opinion about the comets, surely a suggestion that someone beside Galileo saw the lecture as an attack, and an attack not just by Grassi but by the Jesuits.

What had happened? Galileo's erstwhile supporters were now apparently opponents; and Galileo, with the one tone of disputation he knew how to employ, would soon turn opponents into enemies. The lecture of 1618, the first explicit episode in Galileo's relations with the Jesuits after the charge before the Inquisition, takes us back to the crucial period in Rome in 1615-16.

Rome, 1616

What had transpired in Rome? As for the charge of heresy against Galileo, it was quietly set aside. As we shall see, the situation was in fact much more complicated than that statement suggests. Nevertheless, the record of the Holy Office contains nothing that explicitly resolved the charge against him. In a letter to the court in Florence, Galileo reported that he had been successful in convincing the Church of his own integrity.[33] I find the letter puzzling in that Galileo seemed to distinguish his integrity from his Copernican opinions. Nevertheless, Galileo's statement to the court does correspond to the silence of the record about the charge against him.

And the record seems also to treat Copernicanism as a separate issue, for both the Holy Office and the Congregation of the Index took actions on Copernicanism as a result of the charge against Galileo. On 24 February 1616, the group of theologians consulted by the Holy Office found the proposition that the sun stands motionless in the center of the universe to be absurd in philosophy and formally heretical because it expressly contradicts the meaning of several passages of Scripture, and they decided the proposition that the earth rotates daily on its axis and moves in an annual orbit around the sun is also absurd in philosophy and at least erroneous in theology. On 5 March, the Congregation of the Index embodied these decisions in a formal decree which suspended both Copernicus's *De Revolutionibus* and a work by a Spanish theologian Zuniga (which interpreted a passage in *Job* to say that the earth moves) until corrected, and absolutely prohibited a recent book by the Carmelite theologian Foscarini, which had been written in support of Galileo.[34] About any work by Galileo the Congregation of the Index was silent.

The Holy Office and the Congregation were not unaware of Galileo, however. They could scarcely have been unaware of him; his books and the charge of heresy against him had been the immediate occasion of their actions.   On 25 February, the day following their decision that Copernicanism was heretical, the group of theological consultants informed the Holy Office of their judgment on what they called "the propositions of the Mathematician Galileo," and the Holy Office in its turn ordered Cardinal Bellarmino to call Galileo before him and to warn him to give up the Copernican opinion. If Galileo should refuse to obey, the Father Commissary of the Holy Office was instructed formally to order him, before witnesses and a notary, not to hold, discuss or teach the Copernican doctrine in any way, and if Galileo did not acquiesce in the warning, forthwith to imprison him.

This action on 25 February, which focused on Copernicanism rather than Galileo and looked toward the future rather than the past, was the closest approach to a resolution of the charge that had been levelled against Galileo. Cardinal Bellarmino allowed no more time to slip away than the Holy Office itself had. On the next day, 26 February, he called Galileo before him.[35] The interview has been the topic of much discussion because the document that purports to record it was not properly signed. The order possibly given to Galileo that day figured prominently in his trial in 1633, and understandably, since the testimony for it is suspect, there has been extensive discussion about what took place at the interview.

The discussion seems to me largely to ignore the implications of the action itself. Both the Holy Office and the Congregation of the Index were acutely conscious of Galileo. His books, together with the animus that he himself generated in some circles, had led directly to the action taken against Copernicanism, as the theologians' identification of the condemned propositions with him testifies. Those who were informed understood that he stood at the source of the disturbance. Thus, Antonio Querengo, in a letter to Cardinal d'Este, spoke of the decree against Copernicanism as the resolution of "Galileo's disputes."[36] But neither the Holy Office nor the Congregation struck Galileo. Apparently he was immune. Galileo's escape in 1616 has been attributed to the influence of the Grand Duke and of Prince Federico Cesi of the Accademia dei Lincei. This attribution is what I have begun to doubt as I have reflected on the multiple paeans of praise sung to Galileo in that age. They were sung, not just by the Grand Duke and by Cesi, but by the whole class of patrons, that is, by the ruling class, of Italy and of Europe as a whole. Galileo was the illumination of the age. True, he kept advancing paradoxical propositions that challenged the accepted wisdom of the age and common sense itself. Continually he made his patrons nervous, and they felt the need to rein him in. But almost to a man, those who composed the Holy Office, men who by definition belonged to the class of patrons, appear to have been profoundly anxious not to extinguish the light of the age.

Recall that the Pope Paul V, who was repeatedly described as stolidly anti-intellectual, received Galileo in Rome -- received him after the publication of the decree by the Congregation of the Index! -- and assured Galileo of his favor.[37] Recall that when rumors began to circulate that Galileo had been censured by the Holy Office, Cardinal Bellarmino furnished him with an official, signed statement that no such thing had occurred.[38] Recall that in the immediate aftermath of the events of 1616 even conservative Cardinals, such as Borromeo and Aldobrandini, were eager to express their esteem for Galileo, and to receive telescopes and copies of his books from him.[39] Recall that before he left Rome he had begun negotiations through the arch-conservative Cardinal Borgia to supply his method of determining longitude at sea, another fruit of his genius, to the Spanish government, and that during the following two years he remained in constant touch with the Spanish crown on this matter.[40] And recall what seems to me the most revealing indication of all because he was unconscious of its implication, the request that Galileo received from the court in Florence while he was still in Rome in 1616, asking him to stay on until Cardinal Carlo de' Medici arrived, since the court was concerned, "when people of quality dine with him [the Cardinal], that he should have someone present who would be able to please those Lords with his conversation and discourse, for which Their Highnesses judge that you can be the best one possible."[41] It is hard to imagine how we could have a fuller demonstration of the reputation Galileo enjoyed with every segment of the patron class of Italy and of Europe.

If 1616 seemed to indicate that Galileo was immune from threat, must we not say that patronage had made him immune? Such apparently was the conclusion of his enemies. In 1623, Caccini was spreading his opinion around Rome that various "Princes" had defended Galileo from the punishment of the Inquisition, almost that the "Princes" were obstructing the Inquisition and protecting evil persons.[42]

Galileo himself was chastened by the events of 1615-16. He did not quickly forget the terror a denunciation to the Inquisition inspired, and he remained rather quiet for a time. Of course he was not immune from disciplinary action in any absolute sense. He was immune only if he constrained himself within certain limits, and he was well aware of this fact. It seems possible to me that in the late twenties, as he contemplated the enormous gamble the *Dialogue* involved, he reflected anew on the outcome in 1616 and relied again on his apparent immunity. This is speculation, of course, for he left no statement to that effect. The outcome of the denunciation of 1615 is not speculation, however; it is recorded fact.

Galileo's activities in Rome during the six months he was there were recorded well enough that we can also speak of them as facts. By every account he was brilliant, brilliant beyond compare. Everywhere he could be found surrounded by opponents whom he engaged in discourse on the Copernican system and on natural philosophy, "now in one house and then in another."[43] In later years more than one person recalled the impact of his discourse. Virginio Cesarini, a young prodigy of learning in whom the Jesuits had vested great expectations, altered the course of his intellectual life as a result of his discussions with Galileo during these months and took up the study of mathematics and natural philosophy which he had hitherto largely ignored.[44] He chose not to enter the Society of Jesus, but he did become a member of Cesi's *Accademia dei Lincei*. One external observer, who was not a member of Galileo's circle, left an account of a disputation on Copernicanism at the home of Federico Ghisilieri. A whole phalanx of anti-Copernicans were present, attacking him, almost in formation. Before Galileo replied, he made it clear that he understood their position better than they did by strengthening their arguments against himself until they seemed overwhelming, and then he overturned the lot, making his opponents look ridiculous.[45]

A New Relationship

The Jesuits could not have been unmoved by these events. They would have found much on which to reflect. There was the subversion, if one may use the word, of Cesarini. There were the discussions in which they, as the resident intellectuals of Rome, must have participated. It is highly probable that more than one Jesuit, including possibly Orazio Grassi, were present at the debate in the home of Federico Ghisilieri. How exquisitely did Galileo's steadfast supporters enjoy finding themselves the butt of his ridicule? And beyond the realm of personal impact, there was the most important event of all, the outcome of the deliberations of the Holy Office, that is, the demonstration of the position Galileo had established among those who counted. Copernicus was suspended. Zuniga was suspended. Foscarini was prohibited. But Galileo, the cause of all the fuss, the very author of the propositions that the theologians consulted by the Holy Office had been called upon to judge, remained untouched. Here was this new phenomenon on the intellectual scene, the scene the Jesuits had grown accustomed to thinking of as their scene, riding high on the crest of patronage, raised apparently above the ordinary rules. Had he raised himself as well above the authority of the arbiters of Catholic intellectual life?

The Jesuit order was not a monolith, and it is not wise to speak of the order reaching a decision in such matters. Is it possible, however, that influential members of the order -- one thinks immediately of Cardinal Bellarmino, who was the moving agent of the Church's decision to condemn Copernicanism -- decided at that point that it was time to cut Galileo down to size, time to remind him who was in charge?[46] As Grassi would say later, "If the Jesuits knew . . . how to reply to a hundred heretics they would also know how to do it to one Catholic."[47]

Galileo himself was convinced in later years, after his trial, that his troubles had stemmed from the challenge he offered to the Jesuits' domination of Catholic intellectual life. "Having discovered many fallacies in the philosophies commonly taught in the schools now for many centuries," he wrote to Peiresc, "and having communicated some of them and also published some, I have aroused such animus in the minds of those who want themselves alone to be known as learned that, because they are very crafty and powerful, they have known how and been able to grasp the means to suppress what I have found and published and to impede my publication of what remains with me."[48] Interestingly, Descartes apparently assessed the situation in a similar way and justified his own decision not to publish *Le monde* in relevant terms. If he wanted to preserve his tranquillity, he told Mersenne, he could not allow himself to nurse animosities or ambitions. Thus he thought only of instructing himself and rejected the notion of teaching others, "especially those who, having already acquired some credit through false opinions, would perhaps fear to lose it if the truth were discovered."[49]

We almost have to posit a decision at this time by influential Jesuits to reassert their authority in the intellectual realm. Without it, the watershed that 1616 constituted in Galileo's relations with them becomes incomprehensible. No further chapters were added to the saga of Galileo's cordial relations with the order; that era ended abruptly. The close ties that he had formed with Cardinal Alessandro Orsini dissolved with equal abruptness. Orsini had appeared suddenly in Galileo's correspondence early in February. He had displayed, Galileo wrote to the court in Florence, "a singular inclination and disposition to protect and to favor" him, and Orsini appears to have been Galileo's closest companion during the rest of the sojourn in Rome. When Galileo presented his letter of introduction from the Grand Duke to Cardinal Borghese, the Papal nephew, Orsini accompanied him, and though Orsini had received the red hat only in December, after Galileo arrived in Rome, he had been willing to risk Paul V's displeasure by defending Copernicanism before the Papal throne.[50] Galileo addressed the first written version of his treatise on the tides, which he composed at this time and intended as a demonstration from terrestrial phenomena that the earth moves, to Cardinal Orsini.[51] Then, about the end of the sojourn in Rome, as suddenly as he had appeared in Galileo's life, the Cardinal disappeared, never to emerge again. The Jesuit connection offers a possible explanation of the mystery, for the Orsini family had close associations with the order, such that they would later become Scheiner's patrons, and the Cardinal himself was known as a friend of the Society, who would later lay aside the purple in order to become one of them.[52]   One can expect Cardinal Orsini to have been aware of decisions within the order, and to have conformed to them.   And two years after the events of 1616, Grassi delivered his lecture on comets, not a quiet withdrawal in this instance, but a direct challenge to Galileo's authority in science, the foundation of his position.   From this time on, conflict between Galileo and the Jesuits became the norm.

Without pretending that there was not an important divergence of outlook between Galileo and the Jesuits, this analysis suggests that the origin of their conflict was not solely their intellectual differences.   It asks how Galileo, the successful client, impinged on others, and it asks how those with established authority in intellectual life viewed the arrival of a new man whose genius was the more compelling because it enjoyed the support of the patron class.

The rest of the story is quickly told.   Galileo had only one style of controversy.   To Grassi's lecture he replied with a *Discourse on Comets*. The *Discourse* appeared over the name of Mario Guiducci; we know from the manuscript that it was Galileo's composition, and at the time everyone received it as such.   Although the issue of comets had nothing to do with sunspots, Galileo chose to open the *Discourse* with a charge of plagiarism against Scheiner, deliberately couched in the most insulting terms. Scheiner calls himself Apelles, Galileo said, though he does not compare even with a mediocre painter.[53]   Can we seriously wonder that Scheiner became his inveterate enemy? The *Discourse* then proceeded to rip Grassi apart, not yet with the full-throated ridicule of *Il Saggiatore* to be sure, but in a sufficiently humiliating manner nevertheless.

In the reports that Galileo received back from Rome there was no mistaking the reaction now.   It was not Grassi but the Jesuits who were offended, and the word they were using in regard to Galileo was "annihilation."[54]   Grassi replied to the *Discourse* with the *Libra Astronomica* (ascribed to the pseudonymous Lothario Sarsi).   It is instructive to read the *Libra*.   Despite the attack that Galileo had made on him, Grassi replied with restraint, except for one passage.   That one passage offered, with unseemly joy, the wicked insinuation that Galileo remained a closet Copernican.   The insinuation was wholly true, but three years after the condemnation of 1616, it could hardly be received as a friendly gesture. In due time, in response to the *Libra*, Galileo composed *Il Saggiatore*, one of the all time masterpieces of sarcastic invective.   Not even a saint would have received *Il Saggiatore* without hostility, and Grassi has not been nominated for sainthood.   The stage was now fully set for the final drama.

After the tragedy of 1633, two Jesuits who were in a position to know commented on it. Father Grienberger, the successor to Clavius in the chair of astronomy at the *Collegio Romano*, had this to say: "If Galileo had known how to retain the affection of the Fathers of this College, he would have lived gloriously before the world, and none of his misfortunes would have happened, and he would have been able to write as he chose about everything, including the motion of the earth . . ."[55] Grassi's comment on Galileo was still more pointed: "But he has been ruined by himself, by being too infatuated with his own genius and by wholly disdaining that of others; and therefore it is not surprising that everyone conspires to injure him."[56] Both comments seem true to me. And both agree that fully to understand Galileo's conflict with the Jesuits we need to look beyond the intellectual issue that divided them and at the context within which they pursued it, a context in which the system of patronage helped significantly to shape men's actions.

Notes

1.   Magalotti to Guiducci, 7 Aug. 1632; *Le opere di Galileo Galilei*, ed. Antonio Favaro, 20 vols. in 21, (Firenze: Barbèra, 1890-1909), *14*, 368-70.

2.   Cf. Galileo to Diodati, 15 Jan. 1633: "I understand from good sources that the Jesuit Fathers have inserted in the principal heads the conviction that my book is to be detested and is more dangerous to the Holy Church than the writings of Luther and of Calvin . . ." (*Ibid., 15*, 25.)

3.   Cf. Naudè to Gassendi, Ap. 1633, and Micanzio to Galileo, 15 July 1634; *ibid., 15*, 88, and *16*, 109. I could multiply the instances cited if there were need; I am convinced that, if I wished to spend the time, I could multiply them nearly without limit.

4.   Guiducci to Galileo, 21 May 1633; *ibid., 15*, 131.

5.   Bentivogli to Galileo, 21 Sept. 1614; *ibid., 12*, 99.

6.   Gualdo to Galileo, 27 May 1611; *ibid., 11*, 117.

7.   Galileo to Vinta, 19 March 1610; *ibid., 10*, 297-9. The Tuscan court accepted the proposal, and Galileo sent telescopes to a number of rulers in Catholic Europe with letters from the Grand Duke to introduce them.

8.   Faber to Cesi, 11 May 1624; Giuseppe Gabrieli, "Il carteggio linceo della vecchia Accademia di Federigo Cesi (1603-1630)" *Memorie della R. Accademia Nazionale dei Lincei.   Classe di scienze morali, storiche e filologiche, VI, 7.2* (1938), 875.

9.   Gassendi to Galileo, 19 Jan. 1634. *Opere, 16*, 21. See also Diodati to Gassendi, 10 Nov. 1634, Diodati to Peiresc 10 Nov. 1634, and Diodati to Schickhardt, 29 Dec. 1634; *ibid., 16*, 153, 184.

10.   Galileo to Buonamici, 19 Nov. 1629; *ibid., 14*, 52-3.

11.   Castelli to Galileo, 30 July 1638; *ibid., 17*, 361-2.

12.   Nozzolini to Monsignor Marzimedici, 12 Sept. 1612; *ibid., 4*, 289. Galileo to Cesi, 5 Jan. 1613, and Cigoli to Galileo, 1 Feb. 1613; *ibid., 11*, 461 and 476.

13.   *Risposta alle opposizioni*; *ibid., 4*, 727.

14.   *Considerazioni*; *ibid., 4*, 177-8.

15.   Castelli to Galileo, 20 Nov. 1613; *ibid., 11*, 596.

16. *Risposta alle opposizioni*; *ibid.*, *4*, 465. Cf. a passage in Galileo's suggested dedication to the allied "Errori . . . commessi da Messer . . . Coresio," in which he compared himself to a famous painter, probably Andrea del Sarto, whose frescoes in the courtyard of Santissima Nunciata were known to all of Florence, and his critics to clumsy country imitators from the Umbrian town of Montelupo, who are no better than house painters: "And who in our city, if he saw one of the meanest painters of Montelupo running in fury to daub whitewash on the marvelous frescoes of Andrea would not hasten there and with cries and remonstrances and, if they did not suffice, with angry blows prevent this outrageous act? Sig. Galileo has handled this question so superbly that I do not hesitate to say, and you will understand it very well, that Archimedes himself would not have been able to explain it more ingeniously and establish it on more solid foundations, and should a man not oppose one who, ruining everything he touches, attempts to mutilate it?" (*Ibid.*, *4*, 285. It appears to me that in this jibe Galileo is conflating two passages from Vasari's life of del Sarto, one about a monument to him in the church of the Servites made by Raffaella da Monte Lupo, which the superintendents of works in the church mutilated through ignorance, and one about frescoes depicting traitors to Florence that del Sarto painted during the siege of the city, which were later covered with whitewash. Giorgio Vasari, *Lives of Seventy of the Most Eminent Painters, Sculptors and Architects*, ed. E.H. and E.W. Blashfield and A.A. Hopkins, 4 vols. (New York: Scribners, 1897), pp. 293-4 and 298-9.) The literature on Galileo is full of references to Galileo's enemies, but it has not frequently bothered to consider what it was about him that aroused enmity. The provocative display of egotism was a characteristic he never learned to suppress. A decade after the controversy on bodies in water, he wrote the famous passage in the *Assayer*, comparing philosophers to eagles, which can only be read as a self portrait, and one filled with contempt for nearly everyone else: "Perhaps Sarsi believes that all the host of good philosophers may be enclosed within four walls. I believe that they fly, and that they fly alone, like eagles, and not in flocks like starlings. It is true that because eagles are rare birds they are little seen and less heard, while birds that fly like starlings fill the sky with shrieks and cries, and wherever they settle befoul the earth beneath them. . . . The crowd of fools who know nothing, Sarsi, is infinite. Those who know very little of philosophy are numerous. Few indeed are they who really know some part of it . . ." (*Discoveries and Opinions of Galileo*, tr. Stillman Drake, (Garden City, N.Y.: Doubleday, 1957), p. 239. Nearly another decade later, Galileo began the dedication to the *Dialogue* with a passage ostensibly about Ptolemy and Copernicus, which can again only be read as his own portrait of himself: "Though the difference between man and the other animals is enormous, yet one might say reasonably that it is little less than the difference among men themselves. What is the ratio of one to a thousand? Yet it is proverbial that one man is worth a thousand where a thousand are of less value than a single one. Such differences depend upon diverse mental abilities, and I reduce them to the difference between being or not being a philosopher; for philosophy, as the proper nutriment of those who can feed upon it, does in fact distinguish that single man from the common herd in a greater or less degree of merit according as his diet varies." (*Dialogue Concerning the Two Chief World Systems*, tr.

Stillman Drake, (Berkeley: Univ. of California, 1962), p. 3.) What can we call this except hubris? Can we afford to ignore its impact on others if we want to understand important episodes in Galileo's life?

17. Fragments by Galileo in response to Colombe and di Grazia; *Opere, 4,* 443. There may be no need further to establish what is a well known aspect of Galileo, but let me call attention to the notes he made on Antonio Rocco's *Esercitazioni filosofiche,* a reply to the *Dialogue.* Even in private notes Galileo could not curb the violence of his reaction. Thus, "this beast has not fully understood a word of what I say here." Then, "O wicked and totally ignorant!" And ultimately, "blockhead!" "fathead." (*Ibid., 7,* 641, 645, 646, and 668.) After 1633, Galileo did not venture to publish these comments. Before the trial, the system within which he worked tended to encourage him to display his arrogance rather than to conceal it.

18. *Aggiunti* to Galileo, 4 June 1633; *ibid., 15,* 144.

19. Galileo to Castelli, 21 Dec. 1613; *ibid., 5,* 281-8.

20. The records of the Inquisition that concern Galileo are published in *ibid., 19,* 275-421. They include both the 1615-16 episode and trial of 1632-3.

21. Christopher Hollis, *A History of the Jesuits,* (London: Weidenfeld and Nicolson, 1968) p. 128.

22. Martin P. Harney, *The Jesuits in History,* (New York: American Press, 1941) pp. 201-2. David Mitchell, *The Jesuits. A History,* (London: MacDonald, 1980) pp. 57-8. Francois de Dainvillle, *La naissance de l'humanisme moderne,* (Paris: Beauchesne, 1940) pp. 41-2.

23. Dainville, *Naissance,* pp. 75-7. Riccardo G. Villoslada, *Storia del Collegio Romano,* (vol. 66 in *Analecta Gregoriana,* Roma: Universitas Gregoriana, 1954), passim.

24. Dainville, *Naissance,* passim but especially pp. 14-19, 222-8, and 361-71.

25. Galileo to Clavius, 8 Jan. 1588, and Clavius to Galileo, 16 Jan. 1588; *Opere, 10,* 22-5.

26. *Ibid., 1,* 15-177.

27. William Wallace, *Galileo and his Sources. The Heritage of the Collegio Romano in Galileo's Science,* (Princeton: Princeton University Press, 1984). Adriano Carugo and Alistair C. Crombie, "The Jesuits and Galileo's Ideas of Science and of Nature," *Annali dell'Istituto e Museo di Storia della Scienza di Firenze, 8.2* (1983), 3-68.

28. *Opere, 19,* 591-2.

29.   Dini to Galileo, 25 April 1616; *ibid.*, *12*, 174. Galileo to Dini, 16 Feb. 1615; *ibid.*, *5*, 292, 295.

30.   The lecture is printed, in translation, in Stillman Drake and C. D. O'Malley, trs. *The Controversy on the Comets of 1618*, (Philadelphia: Univ. of Pennsylvania, 1960), pp. 5-18.

31.   Rinuccini to Galileo, 2 March 1919; *Opere, 12*, 443.

32.   The line is in the *Assayer* and refers explicitly to a passage in Sarsi/Grassi's *Libra astronomica*. (*Controversy on the Comets*, p. 270.) The tone of Galileo's *Discourse on Comets* can hardly be explained unless we assume a similar reaction to Grassi's original lecture.

33.   As regards the charge against him, Galileo has been assured that "la determinazione essere stata di haver toccato con mano non meno la candidezza et integritá mia, che la diabolica malignitá et iniqua volontá de'miei persecutori." Galileo to Picchena, 6 Feb. 1616; *Opere, 12*, 230. Cf. Galileo to Picchena, 13 Feb. 1616; *ibid., 12*, 233-4.

34.   *Ibid., 19*, pp. 320-3.

35.   *Ibid., 19*, 321-2.

36.   Querengo to d'Este, 5 March 1616; *ibid., 12*, 243.

37.   Galileo to Picchena, 12 March 1616; *ibid., 12*, 247-8.

38.   *Ibid., 19*, 342.

39.   Borromeo to Galileo, 14 July 1617; Giggi (Borromeo's secretary) to Galileo, 26 July 1617; Galileo to Borromeo, 23 Dec. 1617; Giggi to Galileo, 27 Dec. 1617; Ciampoli to Galileo, 21 July 1618; *ibid., 12*, 320, 332, 356-7, 362, and 399-400.

40.   Galileo to d'Argensola, 16 May 1616; *ibid., 12*, 260-1. Related correspondence continued at least until April 1618; *ibid., 12*, 260-384 passim. See especially Galileo to Orso d'Elci, the Tuscan ambassador in Madrid, June 1617, for his account of the beginning of the negotiations; *ibid., 12*, 327-8.

41.   Picchena to Galileo, 19 Feb. 1616; *ibid., 12*, 237. The letter was written in response to Galileo's announcement that he had cleared his own name, but before the decree against Copernicanism and before the extremely negative report on the visit from the ambassador, Guicciardini. By May the court was increasingly anxious to get Galileo out of Rome and back home.

42.   Reported in Castelli to Galileo, 6 December 1623; *ibid., 13*, 156.

43.   Querengo to d'Este, 20 Jan. 1616; *ibid., 12*, 226-7.

44. Cesarini to Galileo, 1 Oct. 1618; *ibid., 12,* 413-15. For another recollection of discussions in Rome see Carlo Muti to Galileo, 7 Sept. 1618 (*ibid., 12,* 411), and for a hostile report that describes the discussions in which he engaged, Guicciardini to Picchena, 13 May 1616 (*ibid., 12,* 259). Francesco Ingoli's tract, *De situ et quiete terrae contro Copernici systema disputatio* (*ibid., 5,* 403-12), which ultimately generated Galileo's *Letter to Ingoli,* arose from one of the discussions in Rome.

45. Querengo to d'Este, 20 Jan. 1616; *ibid., 12,* 226-7.

46. This is similar to the conclusion stated by Giorgio di Santillana after a different analysis. (*The Crime of Galileo,* (Chicago: Univ. of Chicago, 1955), p. 206.

47. The comment was directed specifically at *Il Saggiatore*; reported in Rinuccini to Galileo, 2 Dec. 1623; *ibid., 13,* 153-4.

48. Galileo to Peiresc, 16 March 1635; *ibid., 16,* 235.

49. Descartes to Mersenne, Feb. 1634; *Oeuvres de Descartes,* ed. Charles Adam and Paul Tannery, 12 vols. (Paris: Cerf, 1897-1913), *1,* 282. Cf. substantially the same opinion in Diodati to Bernegger, 6 Jan. 1635; *Opere, 16,* 194-6, and Micanzio to Galileo, 5 May 1635; *ibid., 16,* 264.

50. Galileo to Picchena, 6, 13, and 20 Feb. 1616; *ibid., 12,* 231-2, 235, and 238. Guicciardini to Cosimo, 4 March 1616; *ibid., 12,* 242.

51. *Discorso del flusso e reflusso del mare all'Illustrissimo e Reverendissimo Sig. Cardinale Orsini*; *ibid., 5,* 377-95.

52. Gustavo Brigante Colonna, *Gli Orsini,* (Milano: Ceschina, 1955), p. 257.

53. *Opere, 6,* 48. Drake and O'Malley, *Controversy on the Comets,* P. 24

54. Ciampoli to Galileo, 6 Dec. 1619; *Opere, 12,* 498-9. Cf. Ciampoli to Galileo, 12 July 1619 and Muti to Galileo, 24 Sept. 1619; *ibid., 12,* 465-6 and 492.

55. Galileo quoted a friend in Rome, in Galileo to Diodati, 25 July 1634; *ibid., 16,* 117.

56. Grassi to Bardi;, 22 Sept. 1633; *ibid., 15,* 273.

PATRONAGE AND THE PUBLICATION

OF THE <u>DIALOGUE</u>

The trial of Galileo is one of that small number of events of modern history which appear to be eternally capable of riveting attention. Like the trial of Socrates two thousand years earlier, it has become a symbol of the unending struggle of free inquiry, determined to follow truth wherever it may lead, against the status quo, ever fearful of change. Galileo had published his *Dialogue* in February, 1632. The plague was raging in northern and central Italy at that time, impeding and interrupting communications, and possibly for that reason it was only toward the end of the summer, six months after publication, that Galileo began to hear rumblings of trouble. Then, suddenly, the Church suspended the distribution of the book, and the Holy Office summoned Galileo to Rome. Although he was an old man approaching the age of seventy, who was seriously ill, the authorities nevertheless insisted that he come to Rome in the middle of the winter -- as it was by the time Galileo had exhausted his efforts to evade the summons -- enduring an uncomfortable quarantine, dictated by the plague, along the way, and present himself before the Inquisition. On 22 June 1633 the Holy Office forced Galileo to abjure his Copernican beliefs and sentenced him to imprisonment at its pleasure. To be sure, the Pope immediately modified the terms of imprisonment, so that Galileo was confined first in the Medici palace in Rome, then in the residence of the Archbishop of Siena, and finally (from the end of 1633) in his own home in Arcetri, outside of Florence. Though less unpleasant than a dungeon, house arrest is imprisonment nevertheless, and a prisoner in his own home Galileo remained until the end of his life.

The publication of the *Dialogue* was not the origin of the storm that swirled around Galileo. Always a controversial figure, he had been from the beginning perfectly assured that he possessed the truth and aggressive in asserting as much, and it had thus not taken him long after he emerged into prominence to get himself denounced to the Inquisition in 1615, in effect for Copernicanism. Even before that event his correspondence had begun to mention enemies and persecutors, and after his first brush with the Inquisition the references to them became constant. Despite his enemies and persecutors and his history of controversy, however, without the *Dialogue* there would not have been a trial. Aside from the role the book played in the history of science, the publication of the *Dialogue* was, then, a matter of great importance.

The Decision to Publish

Galileo had been nursing the idea of such a work for a long time. His *Sidereus Nuncius* of 1610 mentioned that he intended to compose a *System of the World*,[1] and he referred to it in the enumeration of works he was planning when he negotiated with the court in Florence about his appointment as mathematician and philosopher to the Grand Duke.[2] Before he could set himself seriously to work on it, however, he found himself denounced to the Inquisition in 1615, and as a result of the charge against Galileo, the Congregation of the Index condemned Copernicanism. During the next several years, Galileo did not talk much about plans to compose a *System of the World*. My enemies, he said ruefully, "have found a way to torment me with impunity, by concealing themselves behind a simulated religion in order to make me appear devoid of the true one."[3]

Then in 1623, Maffeo Barberini was elected Pope Urban VIII. A poet in his own right, who surrounded himself with a circle of literary and artistic friends, Urban was the Pope of the intellectuals. Galileo referred to his election as "this miraculous conjuncture" when it might be possible, if it would ever be, for him to resurrect his plans.[4] Hope is reviving, he wrote to the Pope's nephew, Francesco Barberini, soon to become the powerful Cardinal Francesco Barberini, "hope, which was once quite buried, that we are about to see the most precious learning recalled from its long exile . . ."[5] He journeyed to Rome to express his reverence for the new Pontiff. He was received, and he held long discussions with Urban. We do not know precisely what was said during those discussions, and it is possible that Galileo misinterpreted the assurances he received. What is not in doubt is the fact that Galileo returned vigorously to work on his *System of the World*, and by the end of 1625 he was writing to friends that the book was virtually completed.[6]

A pause then intervened, a pause that lasted about four years. Galileo's letters do not offer an explanation, but it is difficult to believe that anything except the religious issue -- that way his enemies had found to torment him with impunity -- could have been the cause. In 1615, Galileo had been literally tied in knots with anxiety, as well he might have been, and anyone should be able to understand why he would not readily expose himself to those terrors again. He did not lack reminders of them. Thus in 1625 he heard that some unnamed "pious person" had denounced *Il Saggiatore* to the Inquisition, although nothing came of the charge.[7] Since 1616, moreover, Galileo had acquired new enemies, the powerful Jesuit order, who were apt to be less relenting than his earlier ones. The publication of Grassi's reply to *Il Saggiatore* in 1626 reminded him of this fact, and one of Galileo's marginal notes to it indicated clearly enough his perception of the continuing theological threat to his scientific activity.[8] Galileo was still nervous enough in 1628 that he set Castelli to enquiring in Rome about the danger implied by insinuations against him in Grassi's book.[9] We have one forthright statement by Castelli, not long after he had visited in Florence and talked with Galileo, that Galileo waited until Niccolo Riccardi was appointed Master of the Sacred Place (the position of ultimate censor for the Church) to complete the book, so that he could be sure it would be reviewed by a sympathetic reader.[10] Riccardi was appointed Master of the Sacred Palace in 1629, and late in 1629 Galileo did take up the *Dialogue* again and draw it, in very short order, to a conclusion.

His doubts did not evaporate with the completion of the book, for he knew that its publication required a license, and he wanted the license to come from the Papal authorities themselves in Rome. Early in 1630 he set Castelli to work again, enquiring of Ciampoli, Riccardi, and Cardinal Barberini what sort of reception Galileo might expect if he brought the manuscript to Rome. If anything, Castelli's reports showed that Galileo had had good cause to worry, for they contained plenty of references to opposition in the Church to his views. But the reports were not devoid of hope, and Giovanni Ciampoli especially, a close friend of Galileo, high in the hierarchy, with daily access to Urban, urged him to come ahead. If the time was not opportune to overcome all difficulties, he argued, it never would be.[11] Even the encouragement indicated the presence of obstacles, of which Galileo was well aware.

If Galileo had doubts, he was not the only one. The Church was even more filled with hesitations about the new book. One of Castelli's letters contained an account of a conversation with Cardinal Barberini that hinged on the question of whether, in the newly completed manuscript, Galileo assumed that the earth moves. If the earth moves, the Cardinal had said, it must be a star (that is, a planet), and the concept of the earth as a star is opposed to theological truth.[12] It was an ominous report to receive, for the conclusion that the earth is a planet was a necessary aspect of the position Galileo was trying to expound.   Castelli also repeated a comment by Ciampoli about difficult obstacles high in the Church.[13] And in letters to Galileo from this period, responding to things he said in letters that have been lost, there were repeated references to impediments the work was facing.[14] The situation was ambiguous. If there was abundant evidence that influential members of the Church were hostile to the central theme of his book, some things pointed in the other direction. He heard about a conversation Campanella had with the Pope, in which Campanella had complained about how much the prohibition of Copernicus was hampering Catholic efforts to recover Germany. "That was never our intention," Urban had answered with some passion, "and if I had been responsible, that decree would not have been issued."[15] Galileo also heard about a discussion in the presence of Cardinal Francesco Barberini in which someone had made a slanderous reference to Galileo's heretical views.   The Cardinal had cut the speaker off abruptly. He wanted to inform the man that Galileo had no better friends than the Cardinal and the Pope, and that the Cardinal knew Galileo had never entertained such thoughts.[16] The very story was in itself testimony to the ambiguity of the situation, for it indicated both that Galileo had powerful support and that suspicions about his orthodoxy were rife even before anyone had seen the *Dialogue*.

Galileo did bring his manuscript to Rome in the spring of 1630, and he did obtain an imprimatur from Riccardi, the Master of the Sacred Palace. It was an imprimatur with a difference, however, for Riccardi demanded a second review of the manuscript before publication.[17] Galileo's plan at that time was to return to Florence for the final revisions of the book and then to bring it back to Rome where Federico Cesi and the *Accademia dei Lincei* would undertake the publication.   Riccardi demanded that the revised manuscript undergo another review when Galileo brought it back to Rome, before it went to the press. It was clearly an extraordinary step, as both he and Galileo recognized. Then Cesi died, and the outbreak of the plague in central and northern Italy made communications very difficult.   Cesi's death removed Galileo's primary reason for bringing the manuscript back to Rome, and he was convinced that he could not safely send it because of the interruption of transportation caused by the plague. Could he publish it in Florence? Not without the second review. Could the review take place in Florence? Not to Riccardi's satisfaction, though eventually, after much pulling and tugging, he did agree. After the review in Florence, when Galileo thought that he had complied with every demand, he still needed an official instruction from Riccardi to the Inquisitor in Florence that he might proceed to license the book. The order would not come, and by spring Galileo was nearly wild with exasperation.[18] From Riccardi's statements, it is clear that the problem was not Galileo's compliance, but unhappiness with the book itself, at the highest level.[19] Finally, by invoking a vigorous intervention of the Grand Duke, to whom the volume was to be dedicated, Galileo obtained the order he needed, but with it came very explicit instructions about what the preface and the conclusion must say. The preface and the conclusion, which were to indicate the intention and thrust of the book, had already been the subject of extended negotiation. Now Riccardi even drafted a final version of the preface to guide the Inquisitor in Florence, and Galileo tried to avoid trouble by inserting Riccardi's draft into the *Dialogue* verbatim.[20]

Could it possibly be clearer that Riccardi was distressed by the *Dialogue*? Personally, he was favorable to Galileo. As Master of the Sacred Palace, however, he feared a disaster with the book, and he intended to protect himself from it. Riccardi was a prudent man. When the disaster befell, he was able to escape the consequences while others did not. Riccardi was not the only one who feared a disaster. Consider the implications of a phrase in a letter of Niccolini, the Florentine ambassador to Rome, who was also a friend of Galileo and who functioned as intermediary through most of the negotiations with Riccardi. At one point, in forwarding a message, Niccolini took care to specify that he was sending Riccardi's exact words, "in order not to implicate myself in conscience or in reputation by sending either more or less, either better or worse."[21]

Well might they all worry about implicating themselves, for in fact Galileo's conception of the book he had written stood in irreconcilable contradiction to the desires of the Church. The manuscript he had just completed, Galileo wrote to Diodati, constituted "a very full confirmation of the Copernican system, with a demonstration of the emptiness of all that Tycho and others have argued against it."[22] "I consider it [the explanation of the tides] true," he wrote to Buonamici, "and so I consider all those things to which I have joined it."[23] In opposition to Galileo's manifest conviction that he had virtually demonstrated the truth of the Copernican system, the ecclesiastical officials insisted that he play down the theory of the tides. It was Galileo's intention, when he finished the manuscript, to call the book a *Dialogue on the Tides*, an expression of his belief that the phenomena of tides could only be caused by the earth's motion and therefore that tides offered strong physical support to the central affirmation of the Copernican system. The Church would not allow him to mention the tides in the title. It insisted that the book must not appear to offer a demonstration that the Copernican system is true but should merely argue that it is a superior mathematical hypothesis. Galileo must confine himself to showing that the arguments for the Copernican system were known in Rome before the prohibition of Copernicus's book, which was therefore not banned because of any failure to understand heliocentric astronomy.[24] Hence Riccardi's initial demand that he see the preface and the conclusion, which were to contain the required statements about the book's intent, a second time. Even when Galileo gained permission to have the final review in Florence and to publish the book there, the concern about the preface and the conclusion, as I have indicated, remained intense. The fundamental differences of intention about the book were not in fact truly reconciled. As Niccolini told the court in Florence, in a report on an interview with Riccardi, "the truth is that these opinions do not please people here, especially those in high positions."[25]

Thus the very publication of the *Dialogue*, which we tend to accept as part of the natural order of events, poses a problem. We have on the one hand Galileo's hesitations, knowing as he did the reality of the opposition to it, and recalling the torments of 1615. We have on the other hand the reluctance of the Church, knowing well enough that the manuscript was not truly in harmony with its demands. How did the book ever come to be published? My purpose in this essay is to explore how much the system of patronage, which supported all the higher culture in the age of Galileo and supported Galileo himself, can help to illuminate this problem. Before I begin, I want to enter a word of caution. I do not propose that issues connected with patronage constituted the sole factors at work. When complex men in a complex society make important decisions, many strands are twisted into the cord of causation. Among other things, Galileo published the *Dialogue* because he believed it stated the truth, and any account that leaves out so basic a consideration must surely be defective. However, Galileo's conviction that he was expounding truth will not carry us very far in explaining the actions of the Church. And even in Galileo's case it does not seem to me fully to explain his readiness to take what he knew to be an enormous gamble. I ask then the following question: can the internal dynamics of the system of patronage help us to understand -- I say "help us to understand," not "explain" -- the two related decisions, by Galileo and by the Church, that allowed the publication of the *Dialogue*?

Galileo and Patronage

I turn first to Galileo. Until he reached the age of forty-five, Galileo was an obscure professor of mathematics scarcely known beyond the limits of narrow circles in Padua, Venice and Florence.   Then came the telescope and the discoveries in the heavens. With one leap Galileo mounted to the pinnacle of Italian intellectual society. Giovanni Ciampoli called him "the miracle of nature and the splendor of Italy." Virginio Cesarini, like Ciampoli an intellectual who was an important figure in the Papacy, termed him "the unique and true ornament of Italy, and of the sciences."   Such praise was not confined to Italy.   To the Comte de Noailles, the French ambassador to Rome to whom Galileo dedicated the *Discourses on Two New Sciences*, he was "one of the greatest ornaments of our age." Ferdinand III, the Holy Roman Emperor, found him "the true light of our times."[26] Ferdinand spoke after the publication of the *Dialogue*, Noailles after both the *Dialogue* and the *Discourses*. Basically, however, the telescope and the new bodies in the heavens remained the foundation of Galileo's reputation in his own age. It is symptomatic that throughout his life he continued to receive requests for telescopes. Thus in 1629 the King of Spain, Philip IV, decided suddenly that he wanted a telescope. It was not just any telescope that he wanted; it was one of Galileo's. His request passed through the official channels of the court in Florence, on whom the significance of a request from the King of Spain was not lost. At that time, Galileo was just completing the *Dialogue*. Nevertheless, he immediately undertook the preparation of an instrument that would be suitable for a king of Spain.   In due time it arrived in Madrid, and for one short day it was a great success. Alas, on the first night its object lens was broken. The Tuscan ambassador to Madrid wrote to Florence virtually pleading for a replacement -- not next week, now. They could not imagine, he assured the Tuscan court, how much the king desired it, and he kept the mails filled with repetitions of the request until the replacement arrived in Madrid.[27]

The telescope made Galileo a tourist attraction, whom everyone passing through Florence wanted to meet. The desire was not limited to intellectuals; the ruling class shared it fully.   In 1618 the Archduke Leopold of Austria stopped in Florence. Galileo was sick enough to be confined to bed. Never mind; the Archduke visited at his bedside, and a continuing correspondence followed.[28] In 1625, Leopold's brother Charles visited Galileo in his turn, carrying along a jeweled necklace as a gift.[29] That same year the Prince of Poland stopped in Florence for a time as he returned north from Rome, and during his stay paid frequent visits to

Galileo. Eleven years later, as Wladyslaw IV, the same man decided that he too wanted some lenses from Galileo. "Those who enjoy the gift of quality rightly win the affection of Princes," Wladyslaw wrote. "You who through eminence in the sciences have made yourself known to the world, find in Us, among the many who admire you, esteem that corresponds to your worth."[30]

Wladyslaw's words give accurate expression to the mores of the system of patronage. So also does the imprimatur for *Il Saggiatore* by Niccolo Riccardi, the man who became Master of the Sacred Palace in 1629 and was a consultant in 1623 when *Il Saggiatore* was published. The paragraph that he composed is one of the most extraordinary imprimaturs ever penned. "By order of the Most Reverend Father, Master of the Sacred Palace, I have read this work, *The Assayer*; and besides having found here nothing offensive to morality, nor anything which departs from the supernatural truth of our faith, I have remarked in it so many fine considerations pertaining to natural philosophy that I believe our age is to be glorified by future ages not only as the heir of works of past philosophers but as the discoverer of many secrets of nature which they were unable to reveal, thanks to the deep and sound reflections of this author in whose time I count myself fortunate to be born -- when the gold of truth is no longer weighed in bulk by the steelyard, but is assayed with so delicate a balance."[31]

Although Riccardi himself might not, especially in 1623, be regarded as a patron, his words offer a pure statement of the values on which the system stood. Patronage was not a matter of whim or caprice. The system assumed quality and excellence. To patronize second rate work was to advertise oneself to be second rate as well. A patron demonstrated his magnificence by supporting the best. As Wladyslaw said to Galileo, those who enjoyed the gift of quality won the affection of princes. The most prominent benefit of patronage was economic, of course. Galileo was a man without personal wealth. In an age which lacked most of the opportunities we associate with professional science today, he was, after he determined to abandon his university appointment (which for that matter he also owed to patronage), wholly dependent on his patrons, on his stipend from the Grand Duke and on gifts like the jeweled necklace from the Austrian ducal family. But the benefits of patronage were not confined to economic ones. They included prestige (being known among those whose opinion counted as the miracle of nature and the true light of his times) and standing in society (receiving visits from Archdukes and Princes). These benefits were also assumed in the statements of values by Wladyslaw and Riccardi.

We must not, of course, take the statements too literally. Then as now, all things were weighed out in due measure. The same Riccardi, who announced in public that he counted himself fortunate to be born in the age of Galileo, was not, as we have seen, anxious to risk his own neck for Galileo in 1630, and in 1638 he refused to license the publication of a funeral oration for Nicholas Fabri de Peiresc until the author removed comments in praise of Galileo.[32] The same patrons who clucked approvingly at the munificence of the Grand Duke's stipend for Galileo had themselves no intention of existing on so little. With the stipend of a thousand scudi, Galileo received a pension of sixty scudi more from Urban. Cardinal Magalotti, whose income exceeded Galileo's many times, received as his supplement the Bishopric of Ferrara, which was worth four thousand scudi per year.[33] There is no need to insist on these figures. Those in the academic world will comprehend them readily enough, and others will take them as the natural order of things. For all that, the grand phrases were not uttered without meaning, and we shall be ill-advised to think that they were.

Among those who uttered the grand phrases, with reference to Galileo, was Cardinal Maffeo Barberini, as he was called before 1623. Cardinal Barberini happened through Florence in 1612 and was present at the Grand Duke's table when Galileo debated, with an Aristotelian philosopher, the question of why bodies float in water. Barberini displayed sympathy with the position of Galileo, who wrote to him after he travelled on to Bologna. It is a measure of the attention Galileo commanded already in 1612 that Barberini apparently answered his letters, more than once, on the very day he received them.[34] From that time, a special relation existed between the two men.

The events of 1615-16 offered another assessment of Galileo's position. The charge of heresy against him led the Congregation of the Index to condemn Copernicanism, to suspend *De Revolutionibus*, and to prohibit a book by the theologian Paolo Foscarini written in support of Galileo, but the Congregation did not mention Galileo himself or any of his works. The Holy Office warned Galileo privately but not publicly. Galileo's good fortune in avoiding public condemnation has been attributed to the influence of the Grand Duke and of Prince Federico Cesi of the *Accademia dei Lincei*. I would suggest that more than those two were involved. Cardinal Barberini was in Rome at the time, and later he would claim a central role in the decisions of 1616.[35] Nor does Cardinal Barberini exhaust the list. With one exception, no one of importance seemed ready to attack Galileo in 1615-16. The exception was Cardinal Bellarmino, whom everyone accepts as the moving force behind the

Church's action, and even he was concerned primarily to suppress Copernicanism and went out of his way a month after the condemnation to protect Galileo's personal reputation from overt tarnish. No one cared to be known as the person who had extinguished the light of the times. As long as he remained within reasonable limits, it would appear, Galileo had made himself immune.

As I said, in one leap Galileo had mounted to the pinnacle of Italian intellectual society. It is evident that he enjoyed the attention and prestige of his position and that he intended to stay there. Thus some interest attaches to a letter that his Venetian friend, Giovanfrancesco Sagredo, wrote to him in 1613. Sagredo announced his displeasure to hear that Galileo was spending cold nights observing the heavens. Don't expose yourself to the night air, he advised Galileo. Let Mars and Jupiter go their own ways. Pay attention to your health. Take your studies for a diversion. Concentrate on the true philosophy, which is the slave of health and the enemy of ambition. And quit wasting your energy answering ignorant philosophers. For Galileo's sake, he cursed "courts and ambition."[36]

But quit observing the heavens, and quit answering philosophers was what Galileo could not do if he wanted to maintain his status. Consider, for example, his position in 1618 when three comets made their appearance. From Italy, from France, from Germany, including a letter from the Archduke Leopold, Galileo received enquiries about his opinion on the comets.[37] In Rome, Orazio Grassi delivered a lecture on the comets that implicitly attacked Galileo by drawing from them an argument against the Copernican system, with which Galileo had identified his reputation in science. Obviously the topic was fraught with danger in 1618, less than three years after the decree by the Congregation of the Index, but Galileo could not refrain from answering. He composed a *Discourse on Comets* -- his work as we know from the manuscript and as everyone assumed at the time, even though it carried Mario Guiducci's name. The *Discourse* took a major step in the direction of permanently alienating the Jesuits. Grassi (using the pseudonym, Lothario Sarsi) answered the *Discourse* with the *Libra astronomica*. Then four years elapsed before Galileo's *Saggiatore* replied to the *Libra*. His friends, who initially recommended that he remain silent, became increasingly anxious as year succeeded year. His silence was beginning to appear as defeat. Cesi instructed Johannes Faber, to urge Galileo in the name of the *Accademia* that he should respond to the *Libra*, "that it appears that his adversaries on the Comets are prevailing against him."[38] Cesarini entreated him "ardently" to reply to Grassi's publication, "particularly to redeem from the ignorant a false title of victory that they award to that composition."[39] *Il Saggiatore* adequately silenced their anxieties that the light of nature had been extinguished, but no sooner did it appear than Galileo began to receive indications that his admirers were impatient for more. "Here some further new invention of your genius is greatly desired," Ciampoli informed him, "so that if you should decide to have those ideas which you have kept to yourself until now published, I am certain that they would also greatly please Our Lord [Urban], who does not cease to admire your eminence in all things and to retain all the affection held for you in the past."[40] Galileo was all too ready to mention that he had been pondering a discourse on the tides, and he continued to receive similar stimuli constantly. Why did Galileo decide to complete the *Dialogue* and to publish it? Not least because he could not remain the most admired intellectual of the age and not do so.

Perhaps an element of uncertainty in his relations with his primary patron, the Grand Duke, also encouraged Galileo to publish the *Dialogue*. From this distance there appears to have been a distinct coolness between Galileo and the court during the early years of the reign of Ferdinand II. Cosimo died in 1621, leaving a mere boy as his heir and his own mother, Ferdinand's grandmother, the Grand Duchess Christina, as the dominant figure in the court. A pious woman, excessively pious in the view of some, Christina allowed herself to be influenced by the clerical circles in Tuscany that were least friendly to Galileo. Whereas Galileo had been in constant correspondence with the court during his early years as Mathematician to Cosimo, he had almost no similar correspondence during the twenties. When he went to Rome in 1624, the official litter, which usually carried him all the way, dumped him off unceremoniously in Perugia, where he had to call for assistance from Cesi, and when he arrived in Rome he did not stay with the ambassador, in contrast once more with other trips. A passing comment in a letter Galileo received from Geri Bocchineri, the brother-in-law of his son and an official in the government of Tuscany, suggests how strange and dangerous a character the court found him, for all his acknowledged genius. Bocchineri passed on a remark by the Secretary of State, Andrea Cioli, who apparently felt the need to say something inoffensive to Bocchineri about a man related to him by marriage. Even across the span of more than three centuries, the prissiness of this pompous nonentity in the service of a minor Italian state as he commented on the light of the age can almost be tasted. When he had to serve Galileo, Cioli told Bocchineri, he did not think at all about what Galileo was doing but just wrote to him "without any burden on his conscience and without fear of committing sacrilege."[41]

Against the background of this attitude in the court one can appreciate the significance of a challenge to Galileo's primary means of support mounted in 1629, shortly after Ferdinand, though still scarcely nineteen years old, had assumed direction of the government. The challenge came, as it had in 1614, from the religious opposition. The Grand Duke, they pointed out, had been granted extensive income from ecclesiastical sources to maintain a university. Could he, without injury to his conscience, pay a university salary to a man who was explicitly excused from teaching? Galileo drew his stipend from the University of Pisa, where he was a professor of mathematics without obligation either to teach or to reside in Pisa. The challenge was short lived, it is true. The Grand Duke appointed a commission, made up mostly of clergy, but presumably the right ones, which produced a ringing vindication of Galileo and an affirmation of his unique position in the intellectual world, such that he shed more credit on the university than any course of lectures delivered to a limited audience could do.[42] Nevertheless, Galileo's renewed activity on the *Dialogue*, leading to its completion, coincided rather closely with the challenge. It is possible that he felt the need to demonstrate his value to the Grand Duke with a new work dedicated to him.

To insist too much on the situation in Florence, however, is to reduce Galileo's decision to an economic calculation, whereas other features associated with the system of patronage -- such things as prestige and standing in society -- appear to me to have weighed more heavily with him. In 1630, Galileo was more than sixty-five years old. He had been seriously ill much of the time during the previous twenty years, and more recently very seriously ill. His letters suggest that he was convinced he did not have long to live.[43] He wanted to cap his achievement with a great work. If he could not have been unaware that his conception of the work stood in contradiction to the demands of the Church, he apparently hoped that his eloquence would carry the day as it had (at least for him personally) in 1616, and that he would convert the Church, pull it back from the disastrous policy of prohibition, and lead it to embrace the promise of truth. Success in this venture would, of course, also exalt Galileo as the prophet of truth. As one observer said, Galileo saw "how much glory is promised him if he succeeds in casting down an opinion approved by everyone for so many centuries."[44] The words had been spoken in 1616, but they seem to me to assess his motives, both in 1616 and in 1630, correctly. Throughout his life, he had understood opposition to his opinions solely in personal terms. Opponents were envious and malicious -- how frequently the phrase echoed through his correspondence. The triumph of truth and the glorification of Galileo tended to merge into one. Such considerations, operating within the structures defined by patronage, do seem to me to have constituted a major factor in the gamble he took.

Urban as Maecenas

If Galileo as client was moved by the system of patronage, so was Urban as patron. Intellectual circles in Italy looked upon him as one of their own. In the dedication of *Il Saggiatore*, composed almost on the morrow of Urban's election, Cesarini referred to his pontificate as "this universal jubilee of *belles lettres*."[45] A new cultural spring appeared to be dawning, bringing an end to the bleak winter of the Counter Reformation. Urban was the great builder of the baroque age. He was the patron of artists, poets, and scholars, and the friend of the circles in which Galileo moved when he was in Rome.[46] The *Accademia dei Lincei* included in its membership Cesarini and Ciampoli, both of whom held important positions in Urban's pontificate, and both of whom were expected (mistakenly as it turned out) soon to don red hats. Another member was Cassiano del Pozzo, a non-cleric but a man of great influence in the entourage of Cardinal Francesco Barberini, the powerful papal nephew. Shortly after Urban's election, and not long before Francesco Barberini's elevation to the purple, the *Accademia* inducted him into its ranks as well. Thus four members of the *Accademia*, Galileo's closest friends in Rome, with whom he chose to identify by referring to himself as the Academician in the *Dialogue*, stood at the very top of the ecclesiastical hierarchy, and by their presence signaled the promise that Urban's election held.

Immediately after the election, Francesco Stelluti, an official of the *Accademia*, wrote to Galileo that the new Pope was "a particular supporter of learned men, so that we are to have a supreme Maecenas."[47] The word "Maecenas" appears frequently in the literature of patronage. In 1630 Galileo applied it to Ciampoli and heard in response, from Castelli, that Ciampoli "desired that [being known as Maecenas] more than he had desired any precious thing whatever."[48] By every indication, Urban was moved in a similar way by the same ideal. The historical Maecenas had been one of the most powerful men in the immediate entourage of Augustus, the patron of numerous literary figures of the early empire, but especially of Horace and Virgil. In the Renaissance, he became the symbol of the patron, so that his name was converted into a common noun in all of the languages of western Europe during the sixteenth century. Maecenas represented a man who knew what was truly important, a man with everything at his command who nevertheless preferred the life of the mind to power and wealth because he understood that only the things of the mind endure. "Writings inspired by the Muses will eclipse marble monuments," the anonymous author of an elegy to Maecenas had proclaimed: "genius means life, all else belongs to death."[49] As patron, Maecenas participated in the glory and immortality of the artists he encouraged. "Maecenas," Virgil had addressed him in the *Georgics*; "Maecenas, our honour, by just due the chiefest sharer of our fame."[50] All of the evidence suggests that Urban saw himself in such terms, a man raised to power who was demonstrating his magnificence for all time by the conspicuous patronage of activities deemed worthy by right thinking men. "The avidity for glory, that passion of great hearts, arouses him greatly," the Venetian embassy sent to congratulate Urban upon his election reported to its government, "and he is always intent on those things that can elevate his image in the opinion of posterity."[51]

Very early, more than a decade before he wore the tiara, Cardinal Maffeo Barberini established a special relationship with Galileo. If Galileo was anxious that their friendship not dissolve away, Barberini was equally anxious to maintain his connection to the leading intellectual of Italy. In 1620, he inserted three prominent references to Galileo in one of his poems, which became almost a hymn in Galileo's praise, and when Urban's collected poems were reissued after his election, he sent the first presentation copy of the volume to Galileo.[52] To Galileo's extraordinary good fortune, he assisted at the University of Pisa in conferring the doctorate on Barberini's nephew, Francesco, the future Cardinal, in the late spring of 1623, less than two months before Barberini's unexpected elevation to the Papal throne.[53]

Galileo completed *Il Saggiatore* so shortly before Urban's election that publication was still in progress when it occurred. The treatise took the form of a letter addressed to Cesarini, who dedicated the volume, with the author's enthusiastic agreement, to the Pope. Ciampoli read passages from it to Urban, much to the Pontiff's delight.[54] When someone denounced the book to the Inquisition, a special investigation, which cannot have operated without the Pope's approval, arranged simply to kill the charge.[55]

In 1624, Galileo journeyed south to demonstrate his personal reverence for Urban. He arrived in Rome on the evening of 23 April, three hours after sunset. The following morning he had an audience with the Pope that lasted a full hour, and the next day a similar one with Cardinal Francesco Barberini. During the six weeks he was in Rome, Galileo had six personal audiences with the Pope, and he received gifts, including a gold medal, together with the papal promise of a pension for his son Vincenzio.[56] Later on, Urban may have had reservations about the manuscript of the *Dialogue*. It is hardly possible, however, that he could have been more favorably inclined toward Galileo.

Moreover, Galileo had special friends well placed to influence the Pope on his behalf. In 1626, Urban called Benedetto Castelli, Galileo's former student and present friend, to Rome to employ his expertise in hydraulic engineering. Castelli tutored one of the Pope's nephews in mathematics, and through Urban's support received appointment as professor of mathematics at the university in Rome. He made his residence in the Papal palace. Earlier I quoted conversations he held with Cardinal Francesco Barberini, conversations which by themselves demonstrate his familiarity with the inner circle in Rome. There can be no doubt that he exerted his influence on behalf of Galileo, whom he never ceased to regard as his master.

More important even than Castelli was Giovanni Ciampoli, the Secretary of Briefs, who was constantly with the Pope, and who also advised him in favor of publishing the *Dialogue*. In later outbursts, as the trial was beginning to unfold, Urban mentioned the discussions of the book that they had held.[57]

Castelli and Ciampoli were the two special targets of the Pope's anger once the process against Galileo began. Castelli was sent away from Rome during the trial. Perhaps because he possessed technical expertise that could not easily be replaced, he succeeded in holding on to his position, somewhat to his surprise, though it was 1635 before he felt that he had reestablished his former relation with Urban.[58] Ciampoli, on the other hand, lacked competence that could not be replaced, but did possess a sufficient supply of other sins for which to answer. The Pope banished Ciampoli to the provinces and never permitted him to return to Rome. Since Ciampoli did not cease to hope for his restoration to favor, he found it convenient to abandon his correspondence with Galileo. After the trial, Castelli clearly suspected that his correspondence was being watched, and for a long time he wrote only when friends who would carry and deliver the letters were travelling to Florence. Five years passed before he received permission to visit Galileo, and on that occasion the authorities wanted a third person to be present -- one cannot write it without snickering -- lest they conspire together about Copernicanism.[59]

If Castelli and Ciampoli, with their access to Urban, were important, it is evident that the final decision to allow publication of the *Dialogue* lay with the Pope himself.[60] The year that elapsed between Galileo's original presentation of his manuscript in Rome and the final permission to publish it points unmistakably to the same conclusion. From Galileo's point of view, the year appeared as an unconscionable delay. It appears rather different from the Church's point of view. Only fourteen years earlier the Congregation of the Index had pronounced Copernicanism to be a doctrine "ruinous to Catholic truth," and it had prohibited and damned all books teaching the doctrine.[61] The question is not why it took the Church so long to license the *Dialogue*; the better question is why the Church did not reject the manuscript forthwith. Perhaps Riccardi and his associates could not understand Galileo's subtle arguments. The suggestion is inadmissable. Students of no great sophistication understand the arguments readily enough in the 20th century, and in fact the three theologians called upon to examine the book during the trial understood it perfectly.[62] Can we possibly explain the failure to reject the manuscript without reference to the one man who had the authority to override a solemn pronouncement of an official congregation of Cardinals?

When the investigation that prepared for the trial began, Riccardi excused himself by asserting that he had been ordered explicitly by the Pope, through Ciampoli, to license the *Dialogue*. Urban hotly denied his role, and the seventeenth century being what it was, the matter dropped.[63] Nevertheless, Riccardi does appear to have spoken the truth. In general terms, Urban was known as an autocrat who grasped the reins of power jealously and reserved all important decisions to himself, especially during the first decade of his pontificate.[64] During the negotiations that led to the license, constant references to orders from above appeared.[65] Riccardi, who harbored ambitions to wear a red hat and was concerned not to implicate himself in a decision he regarded as perilous, clearly waited until he received orders to proceed. The year's delay, from the spring of 1630 until the spring of 1631, which nearly drove Galileo mad with frustration, was the time it took Urban to realize that he could not bring himself to refuse Galileo's request. Why did the Church, despite manifest reservations about the manuscript, allow its publication? Not least because a Pope, who gloried in his reputation as a Maecenas, was unwilling to place it in jeopardy by saying no to the light of his times.

Altered Circumstances

Then, at the least propitious moment, the whole scene shifted, so that every earlier calculation was rendered false. The prevailing view traces the shift to the crisis in the Thirty Years War.[66] Significant factors, however, are at odds with this view. On the one hand there is the fact that Urban's policy toward France -- and not in any perceptible degree whatever his support of Galileo -- was the source of the friction between the Pope and the Hapsburg powers, and Urban did not reverse his policy for another three years.[67] On the other hand there is the vindictiveness of the Church's attitude toward Galileo that persisted even beyond his death; events in the Thirty Years War seem wholly irrelevant to this attitude.

Urban's special relation to Galileo had made publication of the *Dialogue* possible; perhaps we should look, not only at the level of international politics, but also, and even first, at the personal level for the reversal of his attitude toward his client. In what appears to me more likely to have been the crucial development for Galileo at this time, Ciampoli, Galileo's close friend, whose counsel had helped to win the Pope's approval of publication of the *Dialogue*, fell from grace in April of 1632.[68] Already disenchanted with Ciampoli, Urban allowed himself to be convinced that Galileo was secretly satirizing him through the figure of Simplicio.[69] In the summer of 1632, the scales fell from Urban's eyes -- or so it seemed to him -- and he perceived a new pattern in events around him. Two men whose esteem was vital to Urban's image of himself as Maecenas apparently held him in contempt. And who had been the principal agent in obtaining the license for the *Dialogue*? In a flush of fury, Urban concluded that the whole affair had been what he called "a true Ciampolata."[70]

For Galileo the conclusion was fatal. In his initial outburst, Urban ordered Riccardi to halt distribution of the *Dialogue*. Thus suddenly, near the end of July, more than four months after the first copies had appeared in Rome, Riccardi wrote to the Inquisitor in Florence that Galileo's book had arrived and there was much in it that displeased, so that the Pope and Cardinal Francesco Barberini [i Padroni] intended that it be amended. "Therefore it is ordered by Our Lord the Pope (although only my name is to be used) that the book be withdrawn . . ."[71] That is, the first word of the impending trial that we hear places the Pope rather than the Holy Office at the center of the stage.

During the following months, Urban's fury remained white hot. In September, the Florentine ambassador tried to reason with him about the case. "As we discussed those difficult questions about the Holy Office," Niccolini reported to Florence, "His Holiness exploded in rage, and suddenly said to me that Galileo also had dared to tread where he should not have, and in matters as grave and dangerous as one could imagine in these times." As late as the following March the Pope was still ready to generate enough heat that the ambassador's only thought was to break off the discussion.[72]

Urban's anger with Galileo never did relent. An animus that can only be described as personal pervaded the Church's subsequent treatment of its celebrated prisoner.[73] Though Ciampoli was not condemned to house arrest, the blow that Urban's fury levelled against him was scarcely less lethal. Sent even beyond the provinces, to the farthest backwater of the provinces, to Mont'Alto in the Marches, he languished there, and in a succession of similar metropolitan centers, until his death, far removed from the locus of power and life where, in his ambition, he had imagined his role.

It is significant, nevertheless, that even in altered circumstances, Galileo remained the light of the times, and the set of values on which the system of patronage rested continued to sustain him. A Pope filled with resentment and determined to demonstrate who was master, still chose to handle him with special respect. Although the Holy Office struck him in public in 1633, phrases and themes from his preferential treatment in 1616 echoed through the trial. When Galileo finally arrived in Rome, the authorities allowed him to stay with Niccolini, the Florentine ambassador, for two months. Once the hearings began, they did imprison him, but only for two and a half weeks and not in the ordinary dungeon. Galileo received a suite of three rooms among the chambers of the prosecutors themselves. He had access to the courtyard. His own servant, who could come and go freely, stayed with him. He dined on meals sent in from the Niccolini kitchen.[74] As the ambassador himself remarked, others who were hailed before the Inquisition, including men of title and bishops of the Church, were clapped into prison the moment they set foot in Rome.[75] The record of the proceedings implies that the Papacy, even as it brought Galileo to heel, found itself unhappy to be conducting such a trial, that it wanted to conclude the affair as quickly as possible, that above all it wanted a confession and an abjuration so that it could avoid the shame of condemning the miracle of nature. Perhaps the ultimate ironical statement of the Church's persisting ambiguity toward Galileo came in 1638, when it learned that he was negotiating secretly to communicate his method to determine longitude at sea to the Netherlands. The Papacy, which kept Galileo imprisoned and forbad him even to discuss the Copernican system, still regarded him as the splendor of Italy, who was capable of producing works with which it wished to be associated. Hence the authorities let Galileo know how much they would be displeased if he should put the method of determining longitude in the hands of foreigners and "deprive Italy of the glory of having established, before others, so noble a discovery . . ."[76] In adversity as well as in triumph, Galileo posed a dilemma: they could not live with him; they could not bring themselves to live without him.

Two quotations from the age, related to patronage, serve to summarize the story. One requires an introduction. In 1611, a year after Galileo left Padua, his friend Sagredo, who had been absent when he departed, wrote to express his regret. It was true, Sagredo agreed, that Galileo received a magnificent stipend from a virtuous prince, but in Padua he would have lived as his own master under Venetian liberty. Who could promise, Sagredo asked, that in the tempestuous seas of the court he would not be disturbed by the furious storms of envy?[77] A quarter of a century later, in 1637, when Galileo began to negotiate with the Dutch about his method of longitude, he explained why he was offering it to them. It was the nature of a republic that such a proposal would be considered by qualified men, whereas an absolute prince, who could not understand everything himself, had to rely on the counsel of others, and frequently of men who were not very intelligent. Thus, "that passion which rarely abandons the human mind, that is, the tendency not calmly to witness the elevation of others above oneself, causes the prince, who is badly advised, to despise what is offered, and the one who offered it reaps from it trouble and scorn instead of reward and gratitude."[78] Although Galileo did not mention to the Dutch that he had earlier negotiated with the Spanish about his method, he had, on two different occasions, said substantially the same thing, with the reference to republics and absolute princes omitted, to the Florentine ambassadors in Madrid who represented him.[79] The three statements, virtually repeating Sagredo's sentiments, and especially the one to Reael after the trial, fall little short of explicit expressions of regret that he had not stayed on in Venice and foregone the competition for patronage. The second quotation comes from a letter that Campanella sent to Galileo as the storm began to break. "I observe," he said, "that the more we strive to serve our masters, the more harshly they turn against us and maltreat us."[80] Both quotations remind us that the relation of patronage was a relation of unequals. Galileo had genius. His patrons had wealth and power. Patronage was a device they exploited to enhance their status by conspicuously associating themselves with genius. Never for a moment, as Galileo learned, did they intend that patronage should compromise their position.

Notes

1.   Stillman Drake, tr. *Discoveries and Opinions of Galileo*, (Garden City, N.Y.: Doubleday, 1957), p. 45.

2.   Galileo to Vinta, 7 May 1610; *Le opere di Galileo Galilei*, ed. Antonio Favaro, 20 vols. in 21, (Firenze: Barbéra, 1890-1909), *10*, 351. See also Galileo to Kepler, 19 Aug. 1610; *ibid., 10*, 422.

3.   Galileo to Picchena, 26 March 1616; *ibid., 12*, 250-1.

4.   Galileo to Cesi, 9 October 1623; *ibid., 13*, 134-5.

5.   Galileo to Francesco Barberini, 19 Sept. 1623; *ibid., 13*, 130-1.

6.   Ciampoli to Galileo, responding to a lost letter from Galileo, 28 Dec. 1625; *ibid., 13*, 295.

7.   Guiducci to Galileo, 18 April 1925; *ibid., 13*, 265-6.

8.   In the debate about comets, Grassi argued that mixed bodies containing fire can be transparent, and he cited the passage in *Daniel* in which men were seen in the fiery furnace. In his comment, Galileo's bitterness in his recognition of the theological disadvantage under which he labored flowed over, to the extent that he first confused Grassi's position with his own, and then reversed the two. "Master Lothario, I am not qualified to interpret Scripture, and I believe that you also are not. Therefore I will not deal with your citation until you show me that it has been determined by people of supreme authority that to maintain that flame is transparent is an opinion heretical and erroneous, as repugnant to Scripture. You know where you must appeal; go there and denounce so and so for holding that flame is transparent and insist that this position is contradictory to Scripture. As soon as the declaration is issued, I will not be the second to believe and confess that flame is absolutely transparent." (*Ibid., 6*, 174.)

9.   Castelli to Galileo, 5 Feb., 19 Feb., and 26 Feb. 1628; *ibid., 13*, 391, 393, and 393-4.

10.   Castelli to Galileo, recounting what he had said in a conversation with Riccardi, 9 Feb. 1630; *ibid., 14*, 77-8.

11.   Castelli to Galileo, 23 Feb. 1630; *ibid., 14*, 82. Unfortunately Galileo's letters to Castelli are lost; we have only the replies. See also the two preceding ones, 9 and 16 Feb.; *ibid., 14*, 78 and 80.

12.   Castelli to Galileo, 9 Feb. 1630; *ibid., 14*, 77-8.

13.   Castelli to Galileo, 16 Feb. 1630; *ibid., 14*, 80.

14.   Aggiunti to Galileo, 28 Oct. 1630, Cavalieri to Galileo, 16 Feb. 1631, and Niccolini to Galileo, 10 Aug. 1631; *ibid.*, *14*, 161, 212, and 287. Cf. Galileo to Baliani;, 6 Aug. 1630; *ibid.*, *14*, 130.

15.   Castelli to Galileo, 16 March 1630; *ibid.*, *14*, 87-8.

16.   Buonarroti to Galileo, 3 June 1630; *ibid.*, *14*, 111-12.

17.   From the Inquisition's recital of the event; *ibid.*, *19*, 324-5. See also Riccardi to Clemente (the Inquisitor in Florence), 24 May 1631; *ibid.*, *19*, 327; also Castelli to Galileo, 21 Sept. 1630, and Riccardi to Niccolini, 25 April 1631; *ibid.*, *14*, 150-1 and 254.

18.   Galileo to Cioli, 7 March and 3 May 1631; *ibid.*, *14*, 215-18 and 258-60.

19.   See especially Riccardi to Niccolini, 25 April 1631; *ibid.*, *14*, 254.

20.   Niccolini to Cioli, 16 March and 19 April 1631, Riccardi to Niccolini, 25 April 1631, and Riccardi to Clemente, 24 May 1631; *ibid.*, *14*, 224, 251, and 254 and *19*, 327-30.

21.   Niccolini to Cioli, 19 April 1931; *ibid.*, *14*, 251.

22.   Galileo to Diodati, 29 Oct. 1629; *ibid.*, *14*, 49.

23.   Galileo to Buonamici, 19 Nov. 1629; *ibid.*, *14* 54. Cf. Galileo to Marsili, 20 March 1632; *ibid.*, *14*, 335-6.

24.   Riccardi to Clemente, 24 May 1631; *ibid.*, *19*, 327-30.

25.   Niccolini to Cioli, 19 April 1631; *ibid.*, *14*, 251.

26.   Ciampoli to Galileo, 30 Aug. 1625, Cesarini to Galileo, 12 Jan. 1623, Noailles to Galileo, 20 July 1638, Francesco Piccolomini to Galileo, 5 Feb. 1638; *ibid.*, *13*, 279 and 107; *17*, 357-8 and 276-7.

27.   The first word about the telescope is in a letter of 19 Nov. 1629 from Galileo to Buonamici (in Madrid), who had sent the request to the court in Florence; *ibid.*, *14*, 52-5. Correspondence continued until 26 Nov. 1631, when the new lenses, plus a microscope, arrived; *ibid.*, *14*, 52-310, passim. See especially Borgo's letters of 14 Sept. 1630, telling about the initial arrival of the telescope, and of 13 May 1631; *ibid.*, *14*, 145-7 and 260.

28.   Galileo to Leopold, 23 May 1618, Leopold to Galileo, 11 July 1618, 13 Jan. and 12 Feb. 1619, *ibid.*, *12*, 389-92, 397-8, 435, and 438. See also notes on Galileo's life by his son Vincenzio; *ibid.*, *19*, 595.

29.   Vincenzio's notes; *ibid., 19*, 595. See also Guiducci to Galileo, 18 Oct. 1624, for another honor from Leopold; *ibid., 13*, 217.

30.   Wladyslaw IV to Galileo, 19 April 1636; *ibid., 16*, 420-1.

31.   Stillman Drake and C. D. O'Malley, trs. *The Controversy on the Comets of 1618*, (Philadelphia: Univ. of Pennsylvania, 1960), p. 152. The last line is, of course, a play on the titles of Galileo's *Il Saggiatore*, (*The Assayer*) and Grassi's *Libra astronomica* (*The Astronomical Balance*) to which Galileo was replying.

32.   Bouchard to Capponi, 20 Feb. 1638; *Opere, 17*, 299.

33.   On Magalotti's income, see Andreas Kraus, *Das päpstliche Staatssekretariat unter Urban VIII, 1623 - 1644*, (Rome: Herder, 1964), pp. 71 and 77-8. Castelli reported his appointment as Bishop of Ferrara in a letter to Galileo, 29 April 1628; *Opere, 13*, 421.

34.   Galileo to Barberini, 2 June 1612, Barberini to Galileo, 5 June 1612, Galileo to Barberini, 9 June 1612, Barberini to Galileo, 13 June 1612; *ibid., 11*, 304-11, 317-18, 322-3, and 325.

35.   Niccolini repeated the claim in a letter to the court in Florence, 13 Nov. 1632; *ibid., 14*, 428.

36.   Sagredo to Galileo, 24 Aug. 1613; *ibid., 11*, 553-4.

37.   Cesarini to Galileo, 1 Dec. 1618, Stelluti to Galileo, 25 Dec. 1618, Cesi to Galileo 15 Feb. 1619, Rinuccini to Galileo, 2 March 1619, Bonsi (from Paris) to Galileo, 18 Dec. 1618, Gondi (from Paris) to Galileo, 5 Jan. 1619, Remus (from Innsbruck) to Galileo, 12 Jan. 1619, Leopold to Galileo, 13 Jan. 1619, Roberto Galileo (from Lyon) to Galileo, 16 Feb. 1619; *ibid., 12*, 422-3, 430-1, 439, 443, 428, 432, 433-5, 435, and 440-1.

38.   Cesi to Faber, 28 Aug. 1621; Giuseppe Gabrieli, "Il carteggio linceo della vecchia Accademia di Federigo Cesi (1603-1630)," *Memorie della R. Accademia Nazionale dei Lincei. Classe di scienze morali, storiche, e filologiche, VI, 7.2* (1938), 749.

39.   Cesarini to Galileo, 7 May 1622; *Opere, 13*, 89. See also Faber to Galileo, 18 Jan. 1620; Muti to Galileo, 15 Aug. 1621; Ciampoli to Galileo, 7 Sept. 1621, 18 Dec. 1621, 15 Jan. 1622, and 26 Feb. 1622; Cesi to Galileo, 2 Dec. 1621; *ibid., 13*, 14, 74, 78, 80, 82, 84, and 85-6. Originally, when Grassi's *Libra* appeared, the same group had been as earnest in urging Galileo not to reply. See Stelluti to Galileo, 27 Jan. 1620, and Cesi to Galileo, 4 March 1620; *ibid., 13*, 20-1 and 25. It is relevant, surely, that in his *Lettera a Ingoli*, composed not long after *Il Saggiatore*, Galileo justified his decision to reply to an essay eight years old in identical terms, that is, to vindicate himself from the appearance of defeat. When he was in Rome recently, Galileo said, he found that people took his silence to mean that he was convinced by Ingoli's arguments against the motion of the earth; one person even told him that the arguments were necessary and

insoluble. "And since their being held for such somewhat disturbs my reputation, all the more because in general both those who know and those who don't understand have formed a rather tenuous opinion of my knowledge -- the first because, understanding the small validity of the objections, they nevertheless see me silent, the others because, not being capable of judging by anything but the outcome, they still arrive at the same conclusion [i.e., that Galileo's knowledge is limited] from my silence -- I have found myself forced to reply to your composition . . ." (*Opere, 6,* 510.)

40.   Ciampoli to Galileo, 4 Nov. 1623; *ibid., 13,* 146-7. Recall that the *Accademia* had dedicated *Il Saggiatore* to Urban VIII, who was then still in the early months of his pontificate.

41.   Bocchineri to Galileo, 21 May 1630; *ibid., 14,* 106.

42.   *Ibid., 19,* 487-90.

43.   Among others, see Galileo to Cesi, 15 May 1624, and Galileo to Cioli, 7 March 1631; *ibid., 13,* 178-9, and *14,* 217.

44.   Querengo to Este, 27 Jan. 1616; *ibid., 12,* 229. See also the remarkably similar assessment in Cavalieri to Galileo, 23 Feb. 1630; *ibid., 14,* 83.

45.   Drake and O'Malley, *Controversy on the Comets,* p. 153.

46.   Ludwig von Pastor, *The History of the Popes from the Close of the Middle Ages,* tr. F. I. Antrobus, R. F. Kerr, E. Graf, and E. F. Peeler, 40 vols. (London: Routledge & Kegan Paul, 1924-53), *29,* 408-65. Pietro Redondi, *Galileo eretico,* Torino: Einaudi, 1983), pp. 85-134.

47.   Stelluti to Galileo, 12 Aug. 1623; *Opere, 13,* 121.

48.   Castelli to Galileo, 16 March 1630; *ibid., 14,* 88.

49.   "Elegiae in Maecenatem," *Minor Latin Poets,* (a volume in the *Loeb Classical Library*) tr. J. Wight Duff and Arnold M. Duff, (London: Heinemann, 1934), p. 125. I have modified the translation.

50.   *Virgil's Works,* tr. J. W. Mackail, (New York: Modern Library, 1934), p. 310.

51.   The report of Girolamo Corner, Girolamo Soranzo, Francesco Erizzo, and Renier Zeno, 1625; Nicolo Barozzi and Guglielmo Berchet, eds. *Relazioni degli stati europei lette al Senato dagli ambasciatori veneti nel secolo decimosettimo,* Ser. III, Italia, relazioni di Roma, 2 vols. (Venezia: Naratovich, 1877-8), *1,* 226.

52.   "Adulatio perniciosa," *Maphaei S.R.E. Barberini, postea Urbani PP. VIII. Poemata,* ed. Joseph Brown, (Oxford: Clarendon, 1726), pp. 179-82. There had been an edition of Barberini's poems while he was still a Cardinal, and they were reissued after he was elected Pope. Ciampoli to Galileo, 30 Aug. 1625; Opere, 13, 279.

53.   Maffeo Barberini to Galileo, 24 June 1623; *ibid., 13,* 118-19.

54.   Rinuccini to Galileo, 3 Nov. and 2 Dec. 1623, Ciampoli to Galileo, 4 Nov. 1623; *ibid., 13,* 145, 154, and 146.

55.   See Redondi, *Galileo eretico,* p. 185.

56.   Galileo to Picchena, 27 April 1624, and Galileo to Cesi, 8 June 1624; *Opere, 13,* 175 and 182-3.

57.   Niccolini to Cioli, 5 Sept. and 13 Nov. 1632; *ibid., 14,* 383-4 and 428-9.

58.   Castelli to Galileo, 2 June 1635; *ibid., 16,* 270.

59.   Card. Barberini to Castelli, 16 Oct. 1638; *Ibid., 17,* 393.

60.   This is also the opinion of Karl von Gebler, *Galileo and the Roman Curia,* tr. Mrs. George Sturge, (London: Kegan Paul, 1879), pp. 147-9; of Mario Vigano, *Il mancato dialogo tra Galileo e i teologi,* (Roma: Edizioni "La Civiltaá Cattolica," 1969), pp. 152-62; and of Mario D'Addio, "Considerazioni sui processi a Galileo," *Revista di storia della chiesa in Italia, 38* (1984), 67.

61.   *Opere, 19,* 323.

62.   *Ibid., 19,* 348-60.

63.   Niccolini to Cioli, 23 April 1633; *ibid., 15,* 103-4.   Cf. the account of Giovanfrancesco Buonamici; *ibid., 19,* 410.

64.   Pastor, *History of the Popes, 28,* 51. William Nassau Weech, *Urban VIII,* (London: Constable, 1905), pp. 33-6. Kraus, *Das Staatssekretariat,* passim, especially pp. 2-18. Gebler, *Galileo and the Curia,* pp, 108-9. The Venetian ambassadors to Rome during Urban's pontificate were unanimous in their similar assessment of Urban; Barozzi and Berchet, *Relazioni,* passim.

65.   Elci to Galileo, 3 June 1630, Visconti to Galileo, 16 June 1630, Riccardi to Niccolini, 25 April 1631, Riccardi to Clemente (the Inquisitor in Florence), 24 May 1631; *ibid., 14,* 113, 120, 254; *19,* 327. See also the Inquisition's account; *ibid., 19,* 325. In a later conversation with Niccolini, the Pope virtually agreed that the final order to publish came from him. (Niccolini to Cioli, 5 Sept. 1632; *ibid., 14,* 383.) It is also relevant that in the fall of 1632 it was the Pope himself who insisted that Galileo come to Rome to stand trial; see his note on Galileo's petition to be excused from the trip because of his age and health, a petition referred all the way to the Pope for action, in *ibid., 14,* 410.

66.   Redondi, *Galileo eretico,* pp. 288-94.   Giorgio de Santillana, *The Crime of*

Galileo, (Chicago: Univ. of Chicago Press, 1955), p. 217. D'Addio, "Considera-zioni," p. 80.

67.   The best account of these matters is found in Auguste Leman, *Urbain VIII et la rivaliteé de la France et de la maison d'Autriche de 1631 a 1635*, (Paris: Champion, 1920), in roughly the first half of the book.

68.   Antonio Favaro, "Giovanni Ciampoli," *Amici e corrispondenti di Galileo*, ed, Paolo Galluzzi, 3 vols. (Firenze: Salimbeni, 1983), *1*, 164-8.   Kraus, *Das Staatssekretariat*, pp. 171-2. The biographical sketch of Ciampoli by his secretary, found in the Archivio di Stato, Firenze, in *Manoscritti 752, #6*. The sketch has been published in full in Giovanni Targioni-Tozzetti, *Notizie degli aggrandimenti delle scienze fisiche accaduti in Toscana nel corso di anni LX. del secolo XVII*, 3 vols. (Firenze: Bouchard, 1780), *2*, 102 - 16 (see especially p. 110), and Domenico Ciampoli cites it nearly in its entirely in his biography of his forebear, *Un amico dei Galilei: Monsignor Giovanni Ciampoli*, in his *Nuovi studi letterari e bibliografici*, (Rocca S. Casciano: Cappelli, 1900). Louis Moreri, *Le grande dictionnaire historique*, 18th ed., 8 vols. (Amsterdam: Brunel, 1740), *3*, 419 - 20. (Moreri's *Dictionnaire* appeared originally in 1674.) Niccolini's dispatch of 25 April 1632 in the Archivio di Stato, Firenze, *Mediceo 3351*, f. 324v. (The crucial passage in this dispatch is quoted in the article on Redondi's book in this fascicle.)

69.   If there is any doubt that Galileo and his friends thought that the Pope had been so convinced, see Castelli to Galileo, 12 July 1636; *Opere, 16*, 449-50. On 26 July 1636, in sending on the information in Castelli's letter to Micanzio, Galileo added that the notion he intended to deride the Pope, of which his enemies had persuaded Urban, "was the prime mover of all my troubles." (*Ibid., 16*, 455.) See also the denunciation of Galileo's young disciple, Famiano Michelini, to the Inquisition in 1641, printed in Pio Paschino, *Vita e opere di Galileo Galilei*, (Roma: Herder, 1965), p. 623.   The denunciation quoted Michelini's repetition of what Galileo had told him -- to wit, that the Pope, angered that Galileo had put his opinion into the mouth of Simplicio, and encouraged by Galileo's rivals, ordered the trial.

70.   Niccolini to Cioli, 27 Feb. 1633; *ibid., 15*, 56.

71.   Riccardi to Egidi, 25 July 1632; *ibid., 20*, 571-2. The Inquisition, on the other hand, recorded its first minute in the case nearly two months later, on 23 September; *ibid., 19*, 330. Paschini, *Galileo*, p. 527, and Vigano, *Il mancato dialogo*, pp. 182-6, agree that Urban himself was the driving force behind the trial.

72.   Niccolini to Cioli, 5 Sept. and 13 Nov. 1632 and 13 March 1633; *ibid., 14*, 383-4, 429, and *15*, 68. I had not understood the significance of Urban's anger for my

argument until I read the article by Winifred Wisan, who has insisted similarly on it. Wisan traces Urban's fury to Galileo's covert refutation, in the *Dialogue*, of the very argument about the omnipotence of God that Urban had suggested to him, and that Galileo had then put into the mouth of the same Simplicio in the book's final passage. ("Galileo and God's Creation," *Isis, 77* (1986), 473-86). I find Wisan's presentation persuasive; in my perception our accounts supplement each other without conflicting. Though the thrust of my interpretation places its emphasis on the personal factor rather than on the argument about the omnipotence of God, I have also insisted that I do not regard the factors to which I point as the only ones that were operative.

73.   On these matters see Galileo to Cioli, 23 July 1633; Niccolini to Galileo, 21 Aug. 1633; a petition for pardon from the Ambassador of Tuscany to the Holy Office and Urban's rejection of it on 23 March 1634; Galileo to Diodati, 25 July 1634; Peiresc to Card. Barberini, 5 Dec. 1634 and 31 Jan. 1635; the efforts of the Comte de Noailles to secure a pardon as reported in Castelli's letters to Galileo from 25 Nov. 1634 until 2 May 1637; and a reported initiative of the King of Poland near the beginning of 1637 in Giraldi to Galileo, 26 Dec. 1636, and Peri to Galileo, Jan. 1637; *Opere, 15*, 187-8, 234; *16*, 115-19, 164, 169-71, 202, 532-3; *17*, 16, 70-1; and *19*, 393-4. Eventually, after Galileo became totally blind, the Church, which had earlier peremptorily rejected his requests to reside in Florence in order to be near his physician, did permit him to move into Florence, though still under house arrest, and it is only fair to note that he chose to stay on in Arcetri. (Card. Barberini to Fanano, 6 March 1638; *ibid., 17*, 310-11.)

74.   Galileo to Bocchineri, 16 April 1633, Niccolini to Cioli, 16 April 1633; *ibid., 15*, 88 and 94-5.

75.   Niccolini to Cioli, 16 April 1633; *ibid., 15*, 94-5.

76.   Card. Barberini to Fanano (the Florentine Inquisitor), 19 July 1638; *ibid., 17*, 356.

77.   Sagredo to Galileo, 13 Aug. 1611; *Opere, 11*, 170-2.

78.   Galileo to Reael, June 1637; *ibid., 17*, 104-5.

79.   Galileo to Elci, 13 Nov. 1616, Galileo to Borgo, 1630; *ibid., 12*, 294, and 14, 203-4.

80.   Campanella to Galileo, 22 Oct. 1632; *ibid., 14*, 414-15. I use the translation, which I have modified, of Santillana, *Crime of Galileo*, p. 234.

GALILEO HERETIC:

Problems, as they appear to me, with Redondi's thesis

In reviewing Pietro Redondi's interpretation of the trial of Galileo recently, I did my best to indicate, even in disagreeing, how much I admired the book and how glad I was he had published it.[1] I cannot bring myself to open this essay, in which again I will object to most of the central theses in the book, without stating my admiration for it once more. The book argues that if we want to understand the trial of Galileo we must refocus our 20th century eyes, which are too accustomed to the contrasts of black and white, and learn to perceive the nuances and shadows that were the realities of life in the 17th century. Nothing in that age was what it appeared to be. The external facade of the trial of Galileo was deliberately designed to conceal a reality that differed completely. In pursuing this theme, Redondi reinterprets every major aspect of the trial.

As a historian who has devoted the whole of his professional life to science in the 17th century, I am hardly hostile to the suggestion that we have to accept the age on its own terms. Even less am I hostile to the allied argument, which pervades the entire work, that the transformation of the Christian culture of the Middle Ages into our modern secular culture was a wrenching experience; and however difficult we may find it to appreciate the still vital religious concerns of the 17th century, we cannot hope to comprehend the age if we do not. For all my sympathy with Redondi's position, however, I remain in possession of too many indisputable facts, as I believe them to be, that seem to refuse to fit harmoniously into the new perspective. Needless to say, I am convinced that their refusal to fit is not caused by my inability to immerse myself in the world of the 17th century. Before I proceed to state my reservations, I want to insist on my stance. I do not read lessons to Redondi. He needs none from me. Rather I seek to address him as a peer and to discuss with him an event of epochal proportions which both of us want to understand, the trial of Galileo.

Father Orazio Grassi

Let me begin with the proposition I find least difficult to accept, the rehabilitation of Father Orazio Grassi of the Society of Jesus. Grassi was the Signor Lothario Sarsi (a pseudonym he himself adopted in his reply to Galileo's *Discourse on Comets*) whom Galileo's *Assayer* made into an object of ridicule for all time. Perhaps not for all time, because Redondi has taken the trouble, as no one before him of whom I know had bothered, to look for the real man behind Galileo's corrosive satire. What he finds is a significant intellectual, impressive enough to his own age to have occupied the prestigious chair of mathematics at the Jesuit *Collegio Romano* over an extended period of time and to have been selected as architect of the society's magnificent church of St. Ignatius, which is part of the *Collegio*. I know almost nothing about Grassi apart from what I learned in Redondi's book, and thus cannot bring a truly independent judgment to bear on his assessment. Nevertheless, as I read the account, even though I had not been clever enough to think of investigating Grassi myself, I realized that it had to contain a large measure of truth. The figure of fun that Galileo managed to fob off for Grassi in *The Assayer* could not possibly have been the *Collegio Romano's* professor of mathematics. Whatever the final verdict of the learned community on Redondi's book, surely this aspect of it will continue to survive, a not inconsiderable addition to our understanding of the age.

I do need to enter two caveats, however. Aside from Grassi's achievement in designing the church, Redondi offers no evidence of his capacity. His three works against Galileo (the original lecture on comets, the *Libra astronomica*, and the *Ratio ponderum*) have never appeared to be works of outstanding scientific value, nor does Redondi claim that they are. He cites nothing else. That is, having rehabilitated Grassi, Redondi appears to me to have inflated his significance beyond what the evidence allows. This is one facet of the new perspective, for Grassi's eminence in the Jesuit order is essential to the argument. Thus having presented Grassi and convinced us to take him seriously, Redondi begins (without any justifying argument that I noticed) to refer to him as the "official spokesman of intellectual orthodoxy at the Collegio Romano," "the Society's scientific personality," and the "moral and scientific authority of the Collegio Romano."[2] It appears to me that we have entered here a closed circle of self-confirmation: the new perspective demands that Grassi occupy this status, and the status in turn confirms the new perspective. I am quite prepared to accept Grassi's rehabilitation; without further evidence of his exceptional status I am not ready to step into the circle.

The Accademia dei Lincei

Prince Federico Cesi's *Accademia dei Lincei* also appears radically different in Redondi's treatment. In Rome's "theater of shadows," it becomes a quasi-conspiratorial group, the mirror image of the Society of Jesus, with which it struggled for the soul of Catholicism in the age of the Baroque. Galileo's *Assayer*, Redondi asserts, was the *Accademia's* manifesto.[3] Their opponents, the Jesuits, were the rigorous defenders of Tridentine Catholicism. Let me say in passing that although I do not pretend to expert knowledge about the order, I am uneasy with this characterization of the Jesuits, whose meteoric rise to leadership in Catholic culture from their foundation only three-quarters of a century earlier, appears to me to have been fueled by their capacity to embrace much that was new. Redondi would no doubt reply that there were definite limits to what the Jesuits accepted, and I, of course, would be forced to agree. Nevertheless, *Galileo Heretic* seems to me to present the Jesuits as the intractable opponents of innovation within the Catholic world, and I believe this distorts their record considerably. My concern here is with Redondi's interpretation of the *Accademia*, however. As it happens, I am more confident of myself on this topic. I have studied the entire published record of the *Accademia*, and I need to say that I did not bring away from my reading an image at all similar to the one Redondi offers.[4]

I formed the impression of a small circle, centered always on Cesi, and less an organization than an expression of his aspirations as a patron, which, in direct response to the Prince's personal development, went through a number of definite phases none of which resembled Redondi's image of the *Accademia*. As a youth of seventeen, Cesi organized the *Accademia* initially with two family retainers and a semi-demonic itinerant intellectual from the Netherlands, Jan Eck, who had established himself in Cesi's favor. When Cesi's father understood what was going on, he was so alarmed by Eck's resemblance to Giordano Bruno, who had been executed in Rome less than five years earlier, that he drove Eck not just out of Rome but all the way over the Alps, sent the other two back to their families in the provinces, and brought the first phase of the *Accademia* to an end.

Seven years later, a young man who was no longer a boy and now controlled an estate of his own chose to revive the *Accademia* when he met Giovanni Battista della Porta. To me it seems clear that Cesi hoped to appear before the world as a great patron of learning. In addition to della Porta, he recruited Galileo into his Academy when the Florentine phenomenon descended on Rome after the triumph of the telescope. He also inducted a group of salaried retainers -- Johannes Faber, Johannes Schreck, and Theophilus Müller -- who with Francesco Stelluti from the original group, a man who remained Cesi's household retainer until Cesi's death, worked on a project intimately entwined with the Prince's personal scientific interests. This project, the publication of Nardo Recchi's resume of Francisco Hernandez's pioneering study of Mexican natural history and especially its plants, was always the *Accademia's* central task. The active life of the Academy of the Lynx-eyed belonged to this period. From April to December of 1612, a handful of members in Rome, usually three or four, but five on one occasion, in effect Cesi and a group of retainers, met once a month.

Although regular meetings had tailed off earlier, two traumatic events brought the second phase of Cesi's Academy to an end, the Church's condemnation of Copernicanism in 1616 and Cesi's virtual bankruptcy in 1618. There was an anguished meeting of the *Accademia* after the condemnation; the charges against one of its members had led to the condemnation. Luca Valerio withdrew from the organization, which replied by expelling him. The feature of the meeting that was most revealing of their alarm was the decision also to remove from membership Jan Eck, who was not then in Rome and who had been wholly marginal to the Academy in its second phase, when a mature Federico Cesi had thrown off his tutelage.[5] As that move implies, from the time it was made I found an *Accademia* seeking to avoid suspicion rather than one seeking to be the focus of opposition to official culture.

The second event was even more compelling in the same direction. The Cesi family had risen from obscurity to prominence during the 16th century through service to the church, especially in a succession of cardinalates.[6] To their own misfortune, they quickly acquired the coloration and mores of the older Roman aristocracy. Federico's father was a profligate; Federico had to take over the management of the family estate about 1612. His own aspirations in conspicuous patronage cannot have helped the financial situation much. In 1618 Federico Cesi was forced to abandon Rome, a fact that I did not see mentioned by Redondi, to live on his country estate at Acquasparta. The *Accademia* had exactly one more meeting in its entire existence, which is not, of course, to say that members of the *Accademia* did not meet each other elsewhere on occasion.[7] In 1622 he was forced to sell one of the family's most prized possessions, the great garden of antiquities assembled by an earlier Federico, Cardinal Federico Cesi, to the scion of a newer family rising through the church, Cardinal Ludovico Ludovisi.[8] Four years later, he had summarily to dismiss two clients, Justus Rycke, whom he had encouraged to travel across Europe from Flanders to enter his service, and Johannes Baptiste Winther, because he could no longer pay them. Through the twenties, conflicts within the beleaguered family generated a series of lawsuits against Federico Cesi, which threatened him with instant ruin.

In this situation, as it appears to me, Cesi initiated the third phase of the *Accademia* in which he attempted to use it to shore up his personal position. Largely because of Galileo, the *Accademia* had gained some prominence, and membership in it held significance. In 1618, he inducted three new members, Carlo Muti, son of a prominent Roman family, Virginio Cesarini, also of a prominent Roman family and a rising cleric within the hierarchy of the church, and Cesarini's friend, another rising cleric, Giovanni Ciampoli. In 1621, Cesi added Cassiano del Pozzo, a non-cleric who was intimate with the Barberini, and in 1623, immediately after Urban's election, the Papal nephew, who shortly became the powerful Cardinal Francesco Barberini. Not only did the *Accademia* dedicate Galileo's *Assayer* to Pope Urban VIII, as Redondi emphasizes, but it dedicated to him a short work, *Melissographia* (1626), the first published microscopical observations, an elaborate piece of flattery since its subject, bees, were the emblem of the Papal family, and in 1628 the first installment of the Mexican natural history. Cesi's letters to Cassiano del Pozzo and Cardinal Francesco Barberini in the middle 1620's, the desperate appeals of a desperate man, invoked "the necessity I have of present and immediate help," and offered them "infinite thanks" for their "highly benign protection" in his "unhappy circumstances."[9]

It should be obvious that I cannot fit this collection of evidence into the pattern that Redondi presents of an organization dreaming of challenging the mighty Jesuits and dedicated to overthrowing the official culture. I find it especially revealing that a condensation of the Academy's constitution that Cesi composed in 1624, a document called the *Praescriptiones*, ended with the injunction that Linceans should piously acknowledge the patron saints of the Academy "and all the Blessed Philosophers, especially the divine Thomas Aquinas, the divine Charles Borromeo, as well as the divine Ignatius Loyola, since they always cherish and promote good learning."[10] The *Praescriptiones* stem from almost precisely the time when Redondi has the Linceans conspiring to publish a manifesto of their program for a new Catholic culture, *Il Saggiatore*. The Linceans were the collective personality of Federico Cesi; I find it impossible to imagine him issuing provocative manifestoes of any sort during the final twelve years of his life.

And the notion of *The Assayer* as the collaborative product of the Academy is in conflict with my reading of the record. After Grassi/Sarsi published the *Libra Astronomica* in 1619, the Linceans generally urged Galileo not to reply, not to engage further in so dangerous a contest.[11] Galileo, in contrast, was determined to reply from the beginning, and as the months passed the Linceans in Rome began to hear suggestions that Galileo's silence must mean he had been worsted. At that point they began to urge the desirability of a response upon him -- but a safe one, which answered to the scientific issues and avoided any "satirical and acerbic" style that would aggravate a formidable opponent.[12] I am not aware of evidence that their advice in either form seriously influenced Galileo; what Redondi dubs "Operation Sarsi" appears to me as their reluctant acceptance of Galileo's determination to have at Grassi. The viciously sarcastic assault that Galileo produced could hardly have differed more from their recommendations. I know of no document in which a member of the Academy suggested anything else about *The Assayer's* content.

The manuscript, about which they knew only that Galileo was composing it, arrived in Rome late in October of 1622. There is solid evidence, as Redondi insists, that the treatise passed among the Linceans for reading. Printing had begun by early April, five months after the manuscript arrived. Cesi was in Acquasparta during the entire period. A daughter died in January, and his letters are full of complaints about the family quarrels that continually distracted him. In so far as he was able to turn his attention to intellectual matters, the Mexican natural history commanded his attention far more than Galileo's treatise, if his letters can be taken as a measure.[13] Cesarini and Ciampoli, the other two who figure prominently in Redondi's account, were in Rome, Cesarini suffering from the consumption (again the letters testify) that killed him a year later. Can one seriously imagine that in the brief time available three men, preoccupied with their own pressing concerns and working separately over a treatise concerned with issues on which none was competent, greatly modified a manuscript that became a book of 236 pages? Their letters are explicit in speaking of "some minute adjustments" and a "few words" they had changed.[14] The reader will understand that I continue to believe that *Il Saggiatore* was solely Galileo's manifesto, if indeed one wants to call it a manifesto at all.

Galileo the Atomist

A different Galileo also emerges from Redondi's pages, a Galileo who was not primarily a student of mechanics and certainly not an astronomer, but a natural philosopher who was the foremost agent in the revival of atomism in Europe. Unfortunately, I am again at odds with Redondi on his interpretation of the great Florentine. I must express myself on this matter with care. First, I think one should speak, not of atomism, but of corpuscularianism. The two are similar but not identical. When Redondi first discusses *The Assayer*, he uses the words "particles" and "corpuscles,"[15]   but the new perspective he is urging demands "atoms," i.e. indivisibles, and with a verbal substitution "like an adept card trick" (I use the language he applies to Galileo's *Discourses*)[16] the particles become atoms. Through the rest of *Galileo Heretic*, Redondi holds up *The Assayer* as a polemic for atomism.[17] I do not see clear evidence for more than corpuscularianism, and even that in a tenuous and unsystematic form.

There is a second issue between us which is more important than a choice of words. Although recent scholarship on Galileo's so-called "Juvenilia" threatens to alter our view, the prevailing judgment continues to regard him as a vehement opponent of Aristotelian natural philosophy, and I believe I am correct in saying most scholars agree that Galileo held an inchoate corpuscular or mechanical philosophy of nature, as it is expressed in the passages Redondi quotes.[18] The issue is the centrality of this philosophy in his scientific work. To me, Redondi's evidence for Galileo as atomic philosopher seems thin. In *The Assayer* he finds exactly two passages, the famous one, which no one should try to explain away, on the qualities of bodies and a second that apparently offers an atomic view of light.[19] As Redondi notes, Galileo applied the word "atom" only to light; since he ascribed infinite velocity to the atoms of light and even spoke of their immateriality, I am not convinced that they should be seen as the physical atoms Redondi expounds. In addition, *The Assayer* advanced a kinetic-corpuscular theory of heat.[20] All three instances appear in the discussion about five pages long of a single passage in Grassi/Sarsi's *Libra astronomica*. In a book of 236 pages, I am unable to find here its central theme.

What about the rest of Galileo's career in science? Redondi makes much of the Bologna stone, a mineral that glowed in the dark after being exposed to the sun. He argues that Galileo saw it as a sort of solar sponge and was fascinated by it as a confirming instance of his atomistic conception of light. He may be correct about Galileo's interpretation of the Bologna stone, but the implication that it loomed large in his understanding of nature does not seem to me to find support in the rest of his works and papers. The Bologna stone showed up briefly, and in my view of the evidence superficially, in Galileo's correspondence in 1611. I do not recall another reference to it in his correspondence until 1640 when Fortunio Liceti brought it up again. I do not recall any reference to it in a published work. I have not heard of any manuscripts that discuss it. I need to interrupt here to state that while I have studied Galileo's correspondence, as it is published in the *Opere*, and feel some confidence in discussing it, I have not been a student of his papers. Suffice it to say that no one of whom I know has referred to manuscripts that deal with the Bologna stone and that neither has Redondi done so.

Beyond the Bologna stone (and *The Assayer* of course), Redondi brings up one short passage in the *Dialogue* in which Galileo argues that generation and corruption are accomplished by a simple transposition of parts which, by implication, do not themselves experience change. I do not see how one could deny that this passage assumes a corpuscular, mechanical conception of nature, but I repeat that the issue at stake is not the conception itself but its centrality in Galileo's career. One brief passage in the *Dialogue* is not much. I have very nearly completed my catalogue of the evidence Redondi brings forward. From the correspondence he quotes a note that Galileo jotted down on the margin of a letter from Baliani in 1619.[21] Since this is the only item cited from the correspondence, I would gather he found nothing else. I myself do not remember atomism or mechanical philosophy in general as a feature of the correspondence. I do not see how Redondi's interpretation of Galileo could be true unless Galileo left behind a manuscript record of his efforts to formulate an atomic philosophy of nature. During the past decade there has been an increasingly active exploration of the Galileo manuscripts. Scholars have found that it is possible to reconstruct the stages through which his science of mechanics developed. If anyone has found manuscripts on atomism, I have not heard about them. As I have indicated above, I am not in a position to deny that such exist, but the silence so far appears to agree with the testimony from the correspondence. Redondi himself cites no manuscript evidence. The reader will understand that I have not been able to convince myself that we should see Galileo in Redondi's terms.

Pope Urban VIII

Another important theme of *Galileo Heretic* concerns Pope Urban VIII. In the new perspective, the villain of traditional accounts of the trial, the tyrant of the Vatican, who was unable to adapt to the intellectual world of modern science and insisted instead on humiliating its prophet, becomes the hero who saved Galileo from a fate far worse. In Redondi's theater of shadows, no one acted for selfless motives, of course, and Urban's action in saving Galileo was incidental to his success in saving his own skin. The Thirty Years War appears prominently in the story. From the beginning, Urban's pontificate had pursued a foreign policy that encouraged France as a counterweight to the Hapsburgs, whose dominance of Italy seemed to threaten the independence of the Church. The struggle of France to break the Hapsburg vise constricting her inevitably became entwined with the Thirty Years War, which reached its climax precisely as Galileo's *Dialogue* appeared. In 1631 Gustavus Adolphus, supported none too secretly by France, advanced triumphantly through Germany. During the summer of 1632, the crucial summer for Galileo, he stood just beyond the Alpine passes, seemingly poised to swoop down on Italy. The very survival of the Catholic Church appeared to be in doubt.

On 8 March 1632, in Consistory, Cardinal Borgia, who was also the Spanish ambassador to Rome, read a protest against the Pope in the name of the conservative cardinals. The story of the tumultuous assembly has been told before. Make no mistake -- Redondi tells it extremely well, and his book is worth reading for that episode alone. A liberal Pope, the patron of a cultural thaw after the hard winter of the Counter Reformation, found himself under assault as a Pope who had tolerated the enemies of the faith. There was talk in Rome of summoning a council and implicitly of deposing Urban. In the crisis of his pontificate, Urban saved himself by throwing Galileo to the wolves. He saved himself in a double sense. He separated himself from Galileo and the world he represented; the trial of Galileo rang down the curtain on the cultural awakening and restored the Jesuits to control of Catholic intellectual life. At the same time, by shielding Galileo from more serious charges, Urban as Galileo's patron shielded himself from the accusation that he had sponsored such a dangerous enterprise.

I find difficulties with this account. In regard to the impact of the Thirty Years War on the trial, if one means to argue that 1632 was a period of maximum tension for Urban and that under stress he made decisions he might not have made in other circumstances, I suspect that no one would object to the argument. Redondi is far more explicit than this, however. He makes Urban's cultural policy, as he has described it, and his support of Galileo central features of the conservative rebellion. Thus he implies that Borgia, as a member of the Congregation of the Holy Office, saw Urban's permissiveness, specifically in regard to Galileo, as a grievance.[22] His entire account, in which Urban sacrificed Galileo to appease the conservative powers, appears to me to assume that as a group they saw him as a grievance. I do not see how the argument can stand without that assumption.

But the assumption does not seem to me to have a solid foundation. In his book on *Urbain VIII et la rivalité de la France et de la maison d'Autriche de 1631 à 1635*, Auguste Leman has analyzed the diplomatic correspondence between the Papacy and the major powers of Europe during the period in question and has reproduced many of the dispatches.[23] I have gone through the entire correspondence as he presents it, looking in vain for any mention of Galileo or of any topic remotely connected to Galileo. Why were the Hapsburg powers infuriated with Urban to the extent that the ambassador from Spain read a protest in Consistory? With their unique capacity to see their cause as the will of God, they were angry that Urban was supporting France against them. They were convinced that Urban had secretly allied with France. They demanded the Pope's alliance, and thus the Church's moral support, against France, its financial assistance, in the form of the Vatican treasure and taxation of the Italian church, in the great struggle in Germany, and even the declaration of a crusade. With Gustavus Adolphus loose in Germany, assisted and encouraged by France, Galileo would appear to have been close to the last thing on their mind. On 30 October 1632, as the Holy Office was preparing the trial, the Florentine ambassador to Rome, Francesco Niccolini, reported to Andrea Cioli, the Grand Duke's secretary, that "Sig. Card. Borgia came to find me . . ." Was it perhaps Galileo, the Grand Duke's client, who was on Borgia's mind? If he was, Niccolini entirely forgot that part of the conversation; what he recalled was Borgia's talk of the diplomatic scene and various alliances. On 7 November Niccolini had another long conversation with Borgia, and again, if Niccolini's dispatch was correct, Borgia did not mention anything that concerned Galileo.[24]

In the summer of 1632, the Spanish government convened a Junta to examine its relations with the church. Aldea Vaquero has published in full the memorial of more than one hundred and fifty pages detailing Spain's grievances against Urban's church.[25] To be sure, the memorial concerned itself with the burdens of the church on Spain. Nevertheless, if the Spanish government considered Galileo a grievance, it is difficult to understand why nothing even remotely touching Galileo appeared in the memorial. And Aldea Vaquero's book does not once mention Galileo, although the tension between the Church and Spain is perhaps its central theme. Given the circumstances, I am unable to understand who Urban was supposed to be appeasing, and with what.

Add finally the problem of chronology. Redondi is explicit that after the mini-rebellion in Consistory in March, Urban perforce changed course. As personal revenge, he ordered Cardinal Ludovisi, who had supported the Spanish ambassador, to leave Rome -- "a way of saving papal dignity offended by Borgia -- before surrendering and accepting Spanish and imperial dictates."[26] As the title of Leman's book, with its specification of the years 1631 to 1635, implies, he did not perceive the surrender in 1632. During that summer, the fateful time in Redondi's scenario, Urban was secretly negotiating with the Catholic cantons of Switzerland to take the alpine passes, whereby Gustavus Adolphus might descend on Italy, out of Hapsburg control -- and further infuriating the Hapsburgs when they learned about the negotiations.[27] In the spring of 1633, the viceroy in Naples, convinced that the Pope, in concert with France, was preparing to invade, sought permission to make a preemptory strike into the Papal state.[28] Borgia remained the ambassador in Rome through 1633 while Urban, still outraged at the episode of the previous March, continued to protest his presence. If Urban surrendered to Hapsburg pressure, it was not before 1635. I do not understand what Redondi thinks the Pope was doing with Galileo, a man in whom the Hapsburg powers were apparently uninterested, in 1632?

The interpretation of Urban appears problematic to me, not only from the point of view of the Hapsburgs, but equally from the point of view of the Pontiff himself. If Redondi's account is correct, the Pope's personal attitude toward Galileo remained unchanged even while he was forced to bow to irresistible pressure, and we ought to be able to find evidence of that in the following years. To me, the record appears rather to reveal unremitting vindictiveness in private transactions in which there was no need to maintain a posture for public display. The first word we hear of the coming trial is an order, specifically from Urban, to halt the distribution of the *Dialogue*, two months before any mention of Galileo appeared in the records of the Inquisition, and during the fall of 1632, when the Florentine ambassador tried to discuss the matter with Urban, the Pope as he put it "exploded in rage . . ."[29] As late as the following spring he remained equally furious.[30] Urban reneged on the promise of a pardon that Galileo clearly thought had been made; the record of the Inquisition indicates Urban himself ordered that Galileo be told he would be brought back to a dungeon in Rome if he did not stop asking about the pardon. The Pope even refused the request of an old man prostrate with illnesses to move into Florence where he could be nearer his physician.[31]   These are incontrovertible facts; to me they appear incompatible with Redondi's new perspective.

An important aspect of the argument concerns the banishment from Rome, as Redondi presents it, of all the principal actors in the drama who might have known enough to reveal the Pope's machinations. As part of my general ignorance about Grassi, I did not know that he was transferred out of Rome. The fact does seem to me to support Redondi's position, and I do not have any information that diminishes its importance. In light of other facts that seem at odds with his position, however, I am not prepared to accept Redondi's thesis because of that one alone. The other principal actors do not seem to fit into his pattern equally well. Castelli was not banished from Rome. He does appear to have been sent out of the city during the trial, but he returned immediately following it and spent the rest of his life in Rome. He would have preferred to leave, but the Barberini refused to let him go.[32]

Ciampoli is a wholly different matter. A prominent humanist of the early 17th century who has sunk into the same oblivion as Grassi, Giovanni Ciampoli plays a major role in Redondi's plot. He becomes almost the central figure in Urban's pontificate. Redondi does not shrink from calling Ciampoli the "grey eminence," and such importance does again appear to be a necessary facet of the new perspective.[33] His position of influence allegedly put within reach the goal of the *Accademia dei Lincei* to shape the whole of Catholic culture, and when Galileo fell, he dragged Ciampoli down with him. However, I do not think that Ciampoli was nearly as important as Redondi contends. Instead of standing at the center of Urban's pontificate, he teetered on the periphery, in perpetual danger of being thrown off. He scarcely appears in Kraus' careful study of the inner workings of the Papacy under Urban.[34] It is true that Ciampoli had met Cardinal Maffeo Barberini in Bologna before 1615, but Ciampoli was a dedicated careerist who made it his business to meet everyone of potential importance. His serious contact was not Cardinal Barberini (who had yet to demonstrate that the future belonged to him) but the young Aldobrandini (who as members of an earlier papal family had already arrived) whom he cultivated at Padua, and he first succeeded in entering the central hierarchy of the Church under the Aldobrandini's friends, the Ludovisi.

The biography that his secretary later wrote makes it clear that Ciampoli was always regarded with suspicion in the Barberini papacy as a creature of the Ludovisi.[35] He did not do much to dispel the suspicions.

Ciampoli was an arrogant man. He was not reticent in sharing his opinion that as poets Virgil, Horace, and Petrarch were not in his class.[36] Serving a pope who set a similar value on his own learning, Ciampoli apparently held dangerous views about Urban's intellect; the dangerous views were attached to an active tongue which Ciampoli never bothered to curb. His failure to win a red hat (in itself an indication he was not as influential as Redondi would have it) did not improve his attitude. Scandal mongers later in the century circulated stories that he composed satirical rhymes about the pope and his nephew. When friends urged more caution, he replied that prudence was for those who lacked genius.[37] In addition to Cardinals Aldobrandini and Ludovisi, Ciampoli was close to Cardinal Ubaldini. All three stood with Borgia in the defiance of 8 March 1631 and suffered ostracism as a consequence. There is no doubt that Ciampoli was Galileo's friend, whose influence had been critical in the hard struggle to secure the *Dialogue's* licence for publication, and there is equally no doubt that Ciampoli was primed for disaster.

Inevitably he came under suspicion at the time of Borgia's protest. Ciampoli himself later said that rumors circulated to the effect that he had entered Borgia's palace in disguise the night when the document was in preparation.[38] Perhaps the suspicion in March helped to prepare for Ciampoli's debacle in April, but I have indicated above that Ciampoli had prepared more than enough for it already. In any event, in April the Pope composed a pastoral letter, which he clearly expected to be praised for its eloquence. As Niccolini mentioned in a dispatch of 17 April, Urban distributed pre-publication copies to the cardinals and the diplomatic community for that purpose.[39] Eight days later he had more to report.

> Monsignor Ciampoli, who is considered to be a friend not sufficiently devoted, has fallen entirely from grace, and his latest *faux pas* may well have finished him off. After it had been made quite clear that the Pope intended to compose the recently published pastoral letter by himself, he [Ciampoli] at the same time wrote another version of it that was more elegant and showed it to several people, an act which struck the Pope in the very heart. And as a result, when all of the familiar servants who enter the Papal chambers were told not to enter without giving notice, he then observed that the order was for him alone, for when he wished to carry in some letters to be signed, His Holiness sent the ring [to seal the letters] out of the chamber. And to be brief he [Urban] is now thinking of a way to rid himself of him. But it will not be an absolute disaster if the Pope finally sends him as Nunzio to Naples, as rumor has it.[40]

Urban did not have Naples in mind for Ciampoli. Ciampoli himself indicated that the nunciature to Venice would be acceptable, but Urban did not have that in mind either. By the end of May Ciampoli was ready to settle for the Bishopric of Narni; he let it be known that he would need an income of 2,000 scudi, which Narni was worth.[41]   Urban was not thinking of Narni. In the end, he kept Ciampoli dangling for six months, during which he was not allowed into the Papal presence, until, to get rid of him, he sent him to be governor of Montalto in the Marches. When Ciampoli complained that Montalto was intolerable, Urban found a place that was even worse, Norcia, and transferred him there.[42]   All of this began in the middle of April 1632, well before copies of Galileo's *Dialogue* circulated in Rome.

It does not appear to me that Galileo dragged Ciampoli down. The only question in my mind is whether Ciampoli dragged Galileo down, which would lead to a scenario somewhat at variance with the one Redondi has offered. It is worth noting that Galileo was convinced the source of all his trouble was the Pope's belief that Galileo was satirizing him in the person of Simplicio.[43]   If that was true, his crime was almost identical to Ciampoli's in the Pope's eyes. In fact, those explosions of rage to which Urban treated Niccolini always linked Galileo and Ciampoli. "He [Urban] replied to me with the same heat," Niccolini reported to Florence, "that he [Galileo] and Ciampoli had tricked him, and that Ciampoli in particular had dared to tell him that Galileo intended to do everything that His Holiness demanded and that everything was well . . ." And later in the same conversation the Pope "complained again that he had been tricked by him [Galileo] and Ciampoli."[44] In one outburst, the Pope referred to the whole affair as "a true Ciampolata."[45] It may also be relevant that both were the objects as well of the same remorseless hostility even unto death. In a word, I have not found myself able to accept Redondi's version of the Pope's behavior.

The Trial

And finally, the sum of all the rest, there is the subject of the trial. In Redondi's new perspective, it had nothing to do with Copernicanism. The overt trial concerned with Copernicanism was the subterfuge Urban employed to avoid a trial on the truly serious charge of atomism. Atomism was, or at least influential Jesuits held that it was, incompatible with the doctrine of transubstantiation, which had been defined in Aristotelian terms by the Council of Trent. We confront here the source of Redondi's title, *Galileo Heretic*. In pursuing this theme, Redondi uncovered a new document, hitherto unknown, which he calls "G3," which levelled exactly that charge against Galileo's *Assayer*. At this point I will not need to explain how G3 fits into the general argument of the book. Redondi offers a reasoned argument that Grassi, who repeated the same charge against *The Assayer* in his *Ratio ponderum*, composed G3; and in Redondi's interpretation of the trial, the Jesuit order, following Grassi's lead, stood behind the weighty charge against Galileo that Urban succeeded in shunting to one side. Some Italian critics of Redondi have challenged his assertions that G3 was a formal denunciation to the Inquisition and that Grassi was its author. Whether or not it was a formal denunciation, a question I have no qualifications to judge, it does appear to me that Redondi's argument becomes stronger if Grassi was not the author of G3. The argument requires the issue of the eucharist to have been so serious that every Catholic would have understood any philosophical position incompatible with the Council of Trent's statement of transubstantiation to be beyond the pale of acceptance. However, in Redondi's own terms, two of the theologians on the Pope's special commission appointed late in the summer of 1632 to deal with the Galileo problem were considerably less severe on this supposedly burning issue,[46] and we know from other sources that at much this time, north of the Alps, Descartes and Gassendi, to name no others, both dedicated Catholics determined to remain within the fold, adopted corpuscularian philosophies that embodied the same problem Redondi finds in Galileo's philosophy. If Grassi was the author of G3, we are left with exactly one man who was, at the time, alarmed by the implications of Galileo's philosophy. It is true that Redondi points out another case, in which atomism was involved but Galileo was not mentioned, in the Jesuit college in Prague, at this time.[47] Otherwise, all of his evidence of concern with the eucharist in its relation to a mechanistic philosophy of nature pertains to later decades. I do not find Grassi's concern and the case of Father Arriaga in Prague a sufficient foundation to support the load Redondi wants them to bear.

It also appears to me that Pope Urban and his nephew Cardinal Francesco Barberini must not have understood fully the script Redondi has them compose. Five years after the trial, when Galileo, now blind, again sought permission to move into Florence to be near his physician, the Cardinal wrote to the Inquisitor of Florence that His Holiness did not want to grant the request without knowing from him the nature of Galileo's illness "but much more, whether his return to Florence would give occasion to assemblies, conversations, and discourses from which his condemned opinion about the motion of the earth might possibly be able to revive."[48] And later that year the Pope permitted Castelli, who had not seen his master since the trial, to visit Galileo while Castelli was in Florence, in order to minister to Galileo's soul and to discuss his method of determining longitude at sea [sic!], "but His Blessedness commands, under pain of excommunication, in the full sense and to be incurred without further declaration, the absolution from which His Holiness reserves to himself alone, removing that faculty in this case from the Holy Penitentiary, that he not dare to discuss with the said Galileo the opinion about the motion of the earth condemned by this Supreme and Universal Inquisition."[49] These were private transactions, wholly concealed from view, in which the Pope was free of any need to make a public demonstration. I cannot see how to reconcile them with the thesis that the trial was not about Copernicanism.

I am well aware that I also view the trial of Galileo from a particular perspective. Redondi is bound to find elements awry in my picture, and recalling the power of his book, I have no doubt that I will need to consider his objections with care. In my conception of the intellectual enterprise, understanding advances through informed discussion. Pietro Redondi has laid the entire intellectual community under obligation by setting the trial in a new perspective and arguing his case with such force that the rest of us cannot ignore it. I have done my best in this paper to state my reservations and the reasons for them, but I do not pretend that my perspective has a special sanction that makes it obviously true. There are yet other perspectives as well. Can one sufficiently thank Redondi for his courage in provoking new discussion of an issue so important?

Notes

1.   Pietro Redondi, *Galileo Heretic*, (Princeton: Princeton Univ. Press, 1987); my review is in *Science*, *237* (1987), 1059-60.

2.   Pp. 240, 287, and 328. Cf. also p. 296 for another passage that is not readily quotable without an introduction.

3.   P. 29.

4.   Giuseppe Gabrieli, "Verbali delle adunanze e cronaca della prima Accademia Lincea (1603-1630)," *Memorie della R. Accademia Nazionale dei Lincei, Classe di scienze morali storiche e filologiche*, ser.VI, 2 (1926), 463-512. Gabrieli, "Il carteggio linceo della vecchia accademia di Federico Cesi," *ibid., ser.VI, 7*, (1938-41), 2 vols.

5.   *Verbali, 2*, 497.

6.   Edoardo Martinori, *Genialogia e cronistoria di una grande famiglia umbro-romana i Cesi*, (Roma: Compagnie nazionale pubblicità, 1931).

7.   The meeting was in May 1621. Seven members were present, the largest number that ever attended a meeting. *Verbali, 2*, 501.

8.   Christian Hülsen, *Römische Antikengärten des XVI Jahrhunderts*. (*Abhandlungen der Heidelberger Akademie der Wissenschaften, Philosophisch-historische Klasse*, IV), Heidelberg: Winter, 1917), p. 9.

9.   Cesi to Cassiano del Pozzo, 25 May 1624; *Carteggio, 7.2*, 883-4. Cesi to Cardinal Francesco Barberini, 2 April 1624; *ibid.*, 860-1.

10.   Baldassare Odescalchi, *Memorie istorico critiche dell'Accademia de' Lincei e del Principe Federico Cesi*, (Rome, 1806), pp. 316-17.

11.   Stelluti to Galileo, 27 Jan. 1620 and Cesi to Galileo, 4 March 1620. Cf. LaGalla (who was not a Lincean) to Galileo, 6 March 1620. *Le opere di Galileo Galilei*, ed. Antonio Favaro, 20 vols. in 21, (Firenze: Barbéra, 1890-1909), *13*, 20-1, 25, and 26.

12.   Stelluti to Galileo, 4 April 1620. Cesi to Galileo, 18 May 1620. Ciampoli to Galileo, 18 May, 17 July, and 2 Aug. 1620. *Ibid., 13*, 30-1, 37-8, 38-9, 43-4, 46-7. Cesi to Faber, 28 Aug. 1621; *Carteggio, 7.2*, 749. The words quoted are from Cesi to Galileo, 4 March 1620, when he was still urging Galileo not to reply himself but to find another, perhaps Guiducci, who would do so. Even the substitute was urged to avoid such language. *Opere, 13*, 25.

13.   *Carteggio, 7.2*, 641-792 passim.

14.   Cesarini to Galileo, 12 Jan. and 20 March 1623; *ibid.*, pp. 783-4 and 791.

15.   Pp. 14-16.

16.   P. 19.

17.   See for example p. 281.

18.   William Wallace, *Galileo and his Sources. The Heritage of the Collegio Romano in Galileo's Science*, (Princeton: Princeton University Press, 1984). Adriano Carugo and Alistair C. Crombie, "The Jesuits and Galileo's Ideas of Science and of Nature," *Annali dell'Istituto e Museo di Storia della Scienza di Firenze, 8.2* (1983), 3-68.

19.   *Opere, 6*, 347-50, 352. For Drake's English translation of the passages, *The Assayer* in *The Controversy on the Comets of 1618*, tr. Stillman Drake and C.D. O'Malley, (Philadelphia: University of Pennsylvania Press, 1960), pp. 309-11, 313.

20.   *Opere, 6*, 351-2. Drake translation, pp. 312-13.

21.   P. 16. The letter, with the marginal note, is found in *Opere, 12*, 474-8.

22.   Pp. 244, 257.

23.   Auguste Leman, *Urbain VIII et la rivalité de la France et de la mainson d'Autriche de 1631 à 1635*, (Paris: Champion, 1920).

24.   Archivio di Stato, Firenze; *Mediceo 3352, Carteggio Niccolini a Cioli, July-Dec. 1632*, ff. 354-7 and 392-4.

25.   Quintin Aldea Vaquero, *Iglesia y estado en la España del siglo XVII*, (Santander: Universidad Pontifica, 1961).

26.   P. 232.

27.   *Urbain VIII*, pp. 192-3.

28.   *Ibid.*, pp. 311-12.

29.   Niccolini to Cioli, 5 Sept. 1632; *Opere, 14*, 383-4. See also his report of 13 Nov. on a later meeting; *ibid., 14*, 429.

30.   Niccolini to Cioli, 13 March 1633; *ibid., 15*, 68.

31.   On these matters see Galileo to Cioli, 23 July 1633; Niccolini to Galileo, 21 Aug. 1633; the petition from the Ambassador of Tuscany to the Holy Office and Urban's rejection of it on 23 March 1634; Galileo to Diodati, 25 July 1634; Peiresc to Card. Barberini, 5 Dec. 1634 and 31 Jan. 1635; the efforts of the Comte de Noailles as reported in Castelli's letters to Galileo from 25 Nov. 1634 until 2 May 1637; and a reported initiative of the King of Poland near the

beginning of 1637 in Giraldi to Galileo, 26 Dec. 1636, and Peri to Galileo, Jan. 1637; *Opere, 15*, 187-8, 234; *16*, 115-19, 164, 169-71, 202, 532-3; *17*, 16, 70-1; and *19*, 393-4. Eventually, after Galileo became totally blind, the Church did permit him to move into Florence, though still under house arrest, and it is only fair to note that he chose to stay on in Arcetri. (Card. Barberini to Fanano, 6 March 1638; *ibid., 17*, 310-11.)

32.   See for example Castelli to Galileo, 30 July 1638; *ibid., 17*, 361-2.

33.   P. 48.

34.   Andreas Kraus, *Das päpstliche Staatssekretariat unter Urban VIII, 1623 - 1644,* (Rome: Herder, 1964).

35.   The biographical sketch is found in the Archivio di Stato, Firenze, in *Manoscritti 752, #6.* It has been published in full in Giovanni Targioni-Tozzetti, *Notizie degli aggrandimenti delle scienze fisiche accaduti in Toscana nel corso di anni LX. del secolo XVI,* 3 vols. (Firenze: Bouchard, 1780), *2*, 102-16, and Domenico Ciampoli cites it nearly in its entirely in his biography of his forebear, *Un amico dei Galilei: Monsignor Giovanni Ciampoli,* in his *Nuovi studi letterari e bibliografici* (Rocca S. Casciano: Cappelli, 1900). As perhaps the most generally accessible source, I cite its location in Targioni-Tozzetti, *Notizie, 2*, 110.

36.   Louis Moreri, *Le grande dictionnaire historique,* 18th ed., 8 vols. (Amsterdam: Brunel, 1740), *3*, 419-20. Moreri appears to have been the first to retail this story. His *Dictionnaire* appeared originally in 1674; I have not seen any edition except for the 18th, which I cite here. See also Giulio Negri, *Istoria degli scrittori fiorentini,* (Ferrara: Pomatelli, 1722), p. 275.

37.   Moreri, *Dictionnaire, 3*, 419-20.   Negri, *Istoria*, p. 275.   Apparently the biographical sketch by Ciampoli's secretary was the ultimate source here; Targioni-Tozzetti, *Notizie, 2*, 110.

38.   Ciampoli to Giorgio Cuneo, 7 March 1636; *Lettere di Monsignor Giovanni Ciampoli* (Venice: Pezzana, 1676), pp. 18-20.

39.   *Mediceo 3351,* f. 295.

40.   *Ibid.,* f. 324v. More than a decade later Ciampoli's secretary gave a similar account of his fall; Targioni-Tozzetti, *Notizie, 2*, 110-11.

41.   *Mediceo 3551,* ff. 348 and 449.

42.   Targioni-Tozzetti, *Notizie, 2*, 113.

43.   See Castelli to Galileo, 12 July 1636; *Opere, 16*, 449-50, and Galileo to Micanzio, 26 July 1636, *ibid., 16*, 455.

44.   Niccolini to Cioli, 5 Sept. 1632; *ibid., 14*, 383-4. See also his letters of 13 Nov. 1632 and 13 March 1633; *ibid., 14*, 429, and *15*, 56.

45.   Niccolini to Cioli, 27 Feb. 1633; *ibid., 15*, 56.

46.   Pp. 250-2.

47.   Pp. 240-4.

48.   Cardinal Francesco Barberini to Giovanni Muzzarelli in Florence, 6 February 1638; *Opere, 20*, 582.

49.   Cardinal Francesco Barberini to Muzzarelli, 27 Nov. 1638; *ibid., 17*, 406.